Building God's House

**Seven Strategies for Raising a Healthy Church
The Reuben K. and Mildred T. Hash Story**

By

Dr. Francene Hash

Foreword By Kenneth Copeland

Copyright © 2005 by Dr. Francene Hash

Building God's House—
Seven Strategies for Raising a Healthy Church
by Dr. Francene Hash

Printed in the United States of America

ISBN 1-59781-458-X

All rights reserved solely by the author. The author guarantees all contents are original and do not infringe upon the legal rights of any other person or work. This book or parts thereof and/or cover may not be reproduced in whole or in part in any form, stored in a retrieval system, or transmitted by electronic, mechanical, photocopy, recording, or otherwise, without the express written consent of the author. The views expressed in this book are not necessarily those of the publisher.

Unless otherwise indicated, Bible quotations are taken from the King James Version of the Holy Bible. Emphasis in italics added by author.

Author contact information:
www.fhtmus.com/francene

www.xulonpress.com

Words to the Author from Dr. W. Ronald Hash and Dr. Charles Hash

The Lord gave the word: great was the company of those that published it.

Psalm 68:11

Dr. Francene, *Building God's House – Seven Strategies for Raising a Healthy Church* is a must-read book for all ministers, church leaders, and pastors regardless of whether they are working with a small, medium, or large church. You have done an excellent job in keeping the book interesting and flowing by interweaving the examples of true visionaries, Bishop R.K. and Mother Mildred Hash, and how their leadership principles manifested great success.

Building God's House – Seven Strategies for Raising a Healthy Church is simple enough that you do not want to put it down as you read it, yet profound enough that it is a powerful leadership tool. The book is packed with principles that will help any church grow if they are serious about the work of God.

To pastors throughout the earth, don't put it off. The future of your ministry and vision could be at stake. There is a word from God for you in this book. Watch God bless your ministry above all that you could think!

Thank you, Dr. Francene, for allowing God to use you to be the vessel to usher this magnificent book into the earth for all mankind.

Our family is very proud of you and thankful that you have been able to capture the essence of Mom and Dad's heart.

Bishop W. Ronald Hash, BS, MBA, Ed.D
Love Christian Center, Senior Pastor
East Spencer, North Carolina

Dr. Charles Hash
St. Matthew Word of Life Fellowship, Senior Pastor
Roanoke, Virginia

**"Jesus set the example for true leadership.
You don't drive sheep;
you lead sheep."**

Famous quote by the late Bishop Reuben K. Hash, Sr.

**"God is looking for "stickability".
Stick with Jesus, baby, and He will surely stick with you."**

Famous quote by Mother Mildred Hash.

Table of Contents

Foreword from Dr. Kenneth Copeland xiii
Introduction xv

Chapter One - Strategy One -
   Understand God's Vision for the Church 19

    God Starts With the End in View..19
    Implications for Church Leaders 30
    Principles of Vision..32

    God's Vision in a Man's Heart – the Reuben K. and
    Mildred T. Hash Sr. Story 35
    A Situation to Redeem..36
    Bishop Hash: An Agent of Change.....................................38
    The Call and Vision 43
    Mother Hash: Partner in the Vision 47
    The Visit to Tulsa, Oklahoma 49
    What to Do With the Vision of God in Your Heart............49

Chapter Two - Strategy Two -
   Build People: the Heartbeat of God's Vision 53

    Place the People at the Center of the Vision......................53
    Teach the People God's Word...60

  A School of Ministry..62
  Understanding the Purpose of Ministry 65
  The Principle of Giving..65
  Giving Spiritual Gifts to God......................................66

 Motivate the People to Catch the Vision 69
 Develop the People's Talents. 71
 Develop the People's Character 72
 Counsel the People by God's Word 74
 Develop the People into Leaders 75
 A Balanced Lifestyle.. 79

Chapter Three - Strategy Three -
Organize for the Vision..83
 Identify Leadership for the Vision 83
 Old Testament Foundations 84
 New Testament Continuation of the Principle 85

  Develop Church Ministries 87

   Children's and Youth Ministry 87
   Men's and Women's Ministry..................................88
   Family Enrichment Ministry 90
   Bridge the Gap Between Your Church
    and Your Community......................................90

  Develop a Vibrant Helps Ministry 92

   Gifts in the Church...93
   The Age of Technology..94
   Human Resource Office for Staff and
    Volunteers..94
   Training and Operations Manuals.......................95

  Enhance Your Administrative Support 95

   Membership Tracking Systems 96

Administrative Procedures 97
Powerful Leadership Meetings 98
Financial Systems and Accountability 100
Church Public Relations 101
Communication Center 102
No Gimmicks, No Tricks 102
Profit Centers. 103
The Capital Fund Raising Department 105
The Business Owners in the Church 106
Community Enhancement Services 106
The Power of Recognition and Appreciation 107

Chapter Four - Strategy Four -
Mobilize Your Church to Pray
"Power for the Vision" 109

Establish the Foundation 109
How to Mobilize the Whole Church to Pray 109
The Value of the Senior Members 116
Mildred T. Hash Mother's Board 117
The Sensational Seniors Fellowship 117
Bishop Hash's Strategy for Prayer 118

The Power of Prayer Class 118
Midnight and All Night Prayer Vigils 119
National Prayer Ministry Staffing 119
Community Prayer and Fasting Day 119

Chapter Five - Strategy Five -
Evangelize for Church Growth 123

Lifestyle Evangelism 123
Generational Curses and Blessings 127
Evangelism and Discipleship Classes 136
Accommodating Growth: Building a Bigger Sanctuary 136
Mother Hash, the Dreamer 136

Chapter Six - Strategy Six -
Look Beyond Your Congregation **139**

    No Local Church Stands Alone 139
    Collaboration and Affiliations 141
    Bishop Hash's Strategy: The Church of God
        Apostolic Conference 142

    Twelve Steps in Goal Setting 144

        Package the Vision and Stay Focused 145

Chapter Seven - Strategy Seven –
Leave a Legacy **147**

    Handover 147
    Passing On 149
    The Legacy Lives On 150

Appendix **155**

    Quotes of Wisdom by Mom and Dad Hash 155
    Bible References and Footnote 157
    Epilogue 162
    Acknowledgments 167
    About the *Building God's House Resource Book* 169

Foreword from Dr. Kenneth Copeland

There are two main points I would like to make about Dr. Francene Hash's new book, *Building God's House*.

First of all, her first-hand accounts of her mother and dad, Bishop and Mrs. R. K. Hash, are thrilling and inspiring to all of us who have ever lived the life of faith and service to the Lord Jesus. I only wish Dr. Francene had written more about them, but then the book would have been a foot thick and still wouldn't be enough about such people of holiness, faith, love, and courage.

Secondly, this book touches on something that needs to be said over and over to people in ministry. Whether one is building a church, TV ministry, Christian school, or all of the above, the legal structure and diligence to excellence of ministry is second only to the study of the Word and prayers. I've noticed over the almost 40 years I've been in the ministry that the biggest part of what was called persecution by the IRS or other forms of government would have been totally avoided had the ministry's house been in order.

Jesus' ministry was and is a ministry of excellence. Excellence on every level, not only in our living holy lives, but also in conducting our business lives on just as straightforward a holy level of excellence as our spiritual lives. This includes our own personal lives as well.

All one has to do is visit St. Peter's World Outreach Center in

Winston-Salem, NC and see for yourself. I know from first-hand experience the high level of integrity that Bishop R. K., and then later his son Dr. J. C. Hash, have established in this marvelous church outreach. I've preached there. I knew Bishop Hash and I know and love Mother Hash with all of my heart. I know their hearts. Bishop Hash was like a father and Mother Hash is still like a mother to me. They instilled a level of excellence and boldness for what's right in their own children and their spiritual children as well. J. C. and Joyce have carried on with Bishop's foundation. As you can tell by reading this book, Francene is a strong branch of the same tree.

Pick up on the spirit of what Dr. Francene has shared with us here. There's more to it than just one person's ideas about church growth. She is writing from a long and strong heritage of faith and success in the midst of some seemingly impossible situations, I might add.

I really meant it when I said, "Go see for yourself." Read the book. Go visit St. Peter's World Outreach Center. You'll be glad you did. When you get there, tell them Kenneth and Gloria send all their love.

JESUS IS LORD,
Kenneth Copeland

**Building God's House -
Seven Strategies for Raising a Healthy Church
The Reuben K. and Mildred T. Hash Story**

Introduction

*B*uilding God's House – Seven Strategies for Raising a Healthy Church tells the story of the greatest visionaries that I have ever known: my father, the late Bishop Reuben K. Hash, Sr. and my strong, wonderful mama, Mother Mildred T. Hash. As living epistles, they fought to establish ministry operations founded upon the Word of God, line upon line, and precept upon precept.

They introduced changes that the mainstream denominational churches were not ready to receive, and as a result, they suffered much persecution for righteousness sake. They were among some of the patriots and generals who paved the way for the move of God that we are experiencing in our Full Gospel nondenominational churches today.

This book began as a resource tool for successful church operations, but the more I wrote, I realized that the reason that God graced me with the gift of administration was for a bigger purpose. Before I was born, the doctor told my mother, who had birthed eleven children and experienced three miscarriages, that she would die if she had another baby; yet I had to be born. God's purpose for my existence is because of the vision He instilled in the hearts of my mother and father, so it is their story that must be told. I cannot take any glory for the successes that I achieved in my twenty-four years of service, because my purpose is bigger than me.

God placed something on the inside of me that had to be brought to the earth only by me. Although there are many Church Administrators, God called, anointed, and appointed me for a divine purpose. We are all unique and distinctly different with divine purposes from God.

For twenty-four years, God placed me with my mom and dad in their church that once had less than one hundred members, yet it grew to be a very diverse, large membership of over thirty-five hundred people. It is located on a 75-acre campus with 150,000 square feet of building space. I took so much pride in my job and making things run like a well-oiled machine. I was honored with a doctorate degree for my years of effective service in the ministry.

During the twenty-four years of service, I had the opportunity to lead capital campaign teams that raised millions of dollars over and above the general operating budget, developed a volunteer workforce of over eight hundred diligent workers, and coordinated conferences that drew over five thousand people. Each year, the conferences generated millions of dollars in revenue for the Piedmont Triad convention center, hotels, restaurants, and other vendors. We hosted renowned keynote speakers and recording artists such as Dr. Kenneth Copeland, Bishop T.D. Jakes, Dr. Fred Price, Rev. Kenneth Hagin, Sr., Tommy Barnett, Dr. Myles Munroe, Phil Driscoll, and many more.

God has graced me with the honor of writing this book as a message for the body of Christ:

- For Church Administrators all over the world who have sacrificed their hearts and lives to embrace the godly vision of great visionaries.

- For all the great visionaries who know they have heard from God, but have found themselves wandering in the wilderness to the point of questioning God if they really heard from Him and are on the verge of burnout.

- For all of the great generals who have been in God's army but never received the honor and recognition due them.

- As a reminder to pastors, who have achieved large congregations and buildings, to never stop investing in people.

- For all church leaders who are seeking to fulfill their ministry call and have paid the great price of loyalty and dedication to their pastors.

- For all the volunteers in the Helps ministry who have found their purpose and know where they fit in the body of Christ.

Finally, I have written this book for my sister, Delilah Miller, Uncle Marvin, and my late uncles who were my heroes: Bishop George, Elder Clyde, and Elder J.Y. Hash, who all gave their lives for the work of the ministry. They fed more people, raised more children, and kept more people in their homes than most people will ever do.

Hence, I pray that every pastor, administrator, church leader, and helps worker who reads this book, will read it with an anointing and find between the lines of every chapter the answers and direction for your divine purpose in the body of Christ. Take the strategies, principles, and concepts outlined in this book, apply them liberally, and watch your life and your ministry grow!

Dr. Francene

CHAPTER ONE

Strategy One

Understanding God's Vision For the Church

"God Starts With the End in View"

God starts with the end goal in view.

Everyone who feels called to build God's house must understand what it entails so that they are not tempted to imitate what others are doing, and thereby think that they are building a house that is well pleasing to God. There are many large buildings that are called churches; however, they are only brick and mortar when the presence of God is not there. God is the master builder, planner, and strategist. From the foundation of the world, He designed His Church and orchestrated the strategies and principles for His leaders to follow. When God called Moses in Mt. Horeb, He told Moses exactly what the end of his mission would be: to take the people of God from Egypt into the Promised Land to worship Him.

Go, and gather the elders of Israel together, and say unto

them, The LORD God of your fathers, the God of Abraham, of Isaac, and of Jacob, appeared unto me, saying, I have surely visited you, and seen that which is done to you in Egypt: And I have said, I will bring you up out of the affliction of Egypt unto the land of the Canaanites, and the Hittites, and the Amorites, and the Perizzites, and the Hivites, and the Jebusites, unto a land flowing with milk and honey.
>
> Exodus 3:16-17

Moses was to take God's people into the land flowing with milk and honey, according to the promise He made to Abraham. God knew it all from the beginning and He wanted Moses to have no doubt in his mind what the whole mission was about. Starting a journey or a venture without knowing where you are going is disastrous. Otherwise there is no way you can tell if you are going in the right direction and no way to assess when you have reached your destination. God made it clear to Moses why He was calling him.

God always gives His servants clear instructions before He sends them out.

The next illustration establishes this fact and has to do with designing and making Aaron's robe. Here is the story:

> And take thou unto thee Aaron thy brother, and his sons with him, from among the children of Israel, that he may minister unto me in the priest's office, even Aaron, Nadab and Abihu, Eleazar and Ithamar, Aaron's sons. *And thou shalt make holy garments for Aaron thy brother for glory and for beauty.* And thou shalt speak unto all that are wise hearted, whom I have filled with the spirit of wisdom, that they may make Aaron's garments to consecrate him, that he may minister unto me in the priest's office. And these are the garments which they shall make; a breastplate, and an ephod, and a robe, and a broidered coat, a mitre, and a girdle: and they shall make holy garments for Aaron thy brother, and his sons, that he may minister unto me in the

priest's office. And they shall take gold, and blue, and purple, and scarlet, and fine linen.

Exodus 28:1-5

The rest of the chapter describes in *very precise detail* how the robe is to be designed. Nothing has been described in such beautiful and glorious detail as Aaron's robe. From the passage, it is clear that it was not Moses who designed the robe. God placed His creative wisdom and craftsmanship in the hands of able men to fashion His own image design.

> And they shall make the ephod of gold, of blue, and of purple, of scarlet, and fine twined linen, with cunning work. It shall have the two shoulderpieces thereof joined at the two edges thereof; and so it shall be joined together. And the curious girdle of the ephod, which is upon it, shall be of the same, according to the work thereof; even of gold, of blue, and purple, and scarlet, and fine twined linen.
>
> And thou shalt take two onyx stones, and grave on them the names of the children of Israel: Six of their names on one stone, and the other six names of the rest on the other stone, according to their birth. With the work of an engraver in stone, like the engravings of a signet, shalt thou engrave the two stones with the names of the children of Israel: thou shalt make them to be set in ouches of gold. And thou shalt put the two stones upon the shoulders of the ephod for stones of memorial unto the children of Israel: and Aaron shall bear their names before the LORD upon his two shoulders for a memorial. And thou shalt make ouches of gold; And two chains of pure gold at the ends; of wreathen work shalt thou make them, and fasten the wreathen chains to the ouches.
>
> And thou shalt make the breastplate of judgment with cunning work; after the work of the ephod thou shalt make it; of gold, of blue, and of purple, and of scarlet, and of fine twined linen, shalt thou make it. Foursquare it shall be being

doubled; a span shall be the length thereof, and a span shall be the breadth thereof. And thou shalt set in it settings of stones, even four rows of stones: the first row shall be a sardius, a topaz, and a carbuncle: this shall be the first row. And the second row shall be an emerald, a sapphire, and a diamond. And the third row a ligure, an agate, and an amethyst. And the fourth row a beryl, and an onyx, and a jasper: they shall be set in gold in their inclosings. And the stones shall be with the names of the children of Israel, twelve, according to their names, like the engravings of a signet; every one with his name shall they be according to the twelve tribes.

And thou shalt make upon the breastplate chains at the ends of wreathen work of pure gold. And thou shalt make upon the breastplate two rings of gold, and shalt put the two rings on the two ends of the breastplate. And thou shalt put the two wreathen chains of gold in the two rings which are on the ends of the breastplate. [25] And the other two ends of the two wreathen chains thou shalt fasten in the two ouches, and put them on the shoulderpieces of the ephod before it. And thou shalt make two rings of gold, and thou shalt put them upon the two ends of the breastplate in the border thereof, which is in the side of the ephod inward. And two other rings of gold thou shalt make, and shalt put them on the two sides of the ephod underneath, toward the forepart thereof, over against the other coupling thereof, above the curious girdle of the ephod. And they shall bind the breastplate by the rings thereof unto the rings of the ephod with a lace of blue, that it may be above the curious girdle of the ephod, and that the breastplate be not loosed from the ephod.

And Aaron shall bear the names of the children of Israel in the breastplate of judgment upon his heart, when he goeth in unto the holy place, for a memorial before the LORD continually. And thou shalt put in the breastplate of judgment the Urim and the Thummim; and they shall be upon

Aaron's heart, when he goeth in before the LORD: and Aaron shall bear the judgment of the children of Israel upon his heart before the LORD continually.

And thou shalt make the robe of the ephod all of blue. And there shall be an hole in the top of it, in the midst thereof: it shall have a binding of woven work round about the hole of it, as it were the hole of an habergeon, that it be not rent. And beneath upon the hem of it thou shalt make pomegranates of blue, and of purple, and of scarlet, round about the hem thereof; and bells of gold between them round about: A golden bell and a pomegranate, a golden bell and a pomegranate, upon the hem of the robe round about. And it shall be upon Aaron to minister: and his sound shall be heard when he goeth in unto the holy place before the LORD, and when he cometh out, that he die not.

And thou shalt make a plate of pure gold, and grave upon it, like the engravings of a signet, HOLINESS TO THE LORD. And thou shalt put it on a blue lace, that it may be upon the mitre; upon the forefront of the mitre it shall be. And it shall be upon Aaron's forehead, that Aaron may bear the iniquity of the holy things, which the children of Israel shall hallow in all their holy gifts; and it shall be always upon his forehead, that they may be accepted before the LORD.

And thou shalt embroider the coat of fine linen, and thou shalt make the mitre of fine linen, and thou shalt make the girdle of needlework. And for Aaron's sons thou shalt make coats, and thou shalt make for them girdles, and bonnets shalt thou make for them, for glory and for beauty. And thou shalt put them upon Aaron thy brother, and his sons with him; and shalt anoint them, and consecrate them, and sanctify them, that they may minister unto me in the priest's office.

And thou shalt make them linen breeches to cover their

nakedness; from the loins even unto the thighs they shall reach: And they shall be upon Aaron, and upon his sons, when they come in unto the tabernacle of the congregation, or when they come near unto the altar to minister in the holy place; that they bear not iniquity, and die: *it shall be a statute for ever unto him and his seed after him.*

Exodus 28:6-43

There is only one reason why Aaron's robe came out perfectly the way God wanted it.

Moses saw in his mind exactly what God wanted. He did not miss one intricate detail. Moses could not rush to have it designed until he first clearly heard from God what it was to look like.

Since we cannot be sure if Moses had a pen and paper which with to draw the specifications as God spoke, we can assume that he captured in his mind the image of what God wanted Aaron's robe to look like, including all the precise details. Moses understood God's directives so clearly that when he narrated them to the designers, they also caught the image as explicitly as if God Himself told them. The scriptures indicate that Aaron's priestly robe was meant for beauty and glory. God gave the picture; Moses received the picture; Moses described it to the designers, and they made it according to God's specifications. That was splendid! *There was no way this could have happened unless the designers understood exactly what was required of them by God through Moses.*

We cannot build God's house unless we first understand exactly what God wants His house to look like.

Consider how we do that in the natural. For example, we hire an architect to design our homes. We go through the conception and planning process with them; we tell them exactly what we want and they transfer our vision on to paper. Sometimes we even require a three-dimension model of the building before we start building. Why then, without God's master plan, do we assume that we know what to do and can just take off and start to build His spiritual house?

Since we are all familiar with the word *vision,* we will introduce it here. No one can successfully start and complete a project unless one has a vision of what it should look like when it is completed. Vision is not what you do, but rather what you see! According to Webster's Dictionary, *vision* is defined as a divine revelation; an image or imagination; the ability to imagine or foresee what cannot actually be seen; a person or thing of unusual beauty.

The common phenomenon today is that individuals and corporate bodies, including business entities, service organizations, learning institutions, and churches, have their vision as part of their basic tenets. Almost every organization today is identified by its perceived vision.

Over the last fifteen or twenty years, I've found that vision statements for churches and church organizations have not surprisingly many similarities. Churches have the same mandate from the same God for the same inevitable purpose. No vision for any church is sound unless it conforms to the pattern of God's vision. It is important also to note that God will commit Himself to a vision only if that vision follows the pattern He provides in His Word. Because God has not left us in doubt about His will, we need not make assumptions about it.

Any vision, whether personal or corporate, that does not align with God's vision will not have His approval or support because its execution will not bring glory to God. A man's vision will glorify man and God's vision will glorify God. The Spirit of God must birth a vision into our hearts. Therefore, every man or woman must examine their vision to make sure it aligns with God's vision, which then becomes the blueprint of our faith.

Without vision, our faith has nothing to which to add substance.

This chapter is dedicated to the importance of understanding God's vision. Every person who serves God, regardless of their role, should do so with the knowledge and understanding of God's vision and not their own way. We know from the scriptures that God's house refers to the Church, the universal body of Christ.

Even though many of us claim to know that, when it comes to ministry, the Church does not consist of buildings and programs, we often show that we have little understanding of God's vision for His people. To understand God's vision for the Church, we need to examine two very prominent scriptures from Paul's letter to the Ephesians:

> He that descended is the same also that ascended up far above all heavens, that he might fill all things. And he gave some, apostles; and some, prophets; and some, evangelists; and some, pastors and teachers; For the perfecting of the saints, for the work of the ministry, for the edifying of the body of Christ: Till we all come in the unity of the faith, and of the knowledge of the Son of God, unto a perfect man, unto the measure of the stature of the fulness of Christ: That we henceforth be no more children, tossed to and fro, and carried about with every wind of doctrine, by the sleight of men, and cunning craftiness, whereby they lie in wait to deceive; But speaking the truth in love, may grow up into him in all things, which is the head, even Christ: From whom the whole body fitly joined together and compacted by that which every joint supplieth, according to the effectual working in the measure of every part, maketh increase of the body unto the edifying of itself in love.
>
> Ephesians 4:10-16

> Husbands, love your wives, even as Christ also loved the church, and gave himself for it; That he might sanctify and cleanse it with the washing of water by the word, That he might present it to himself a glorious church, not having spot, or wrinkle, or any such thing; but that it should be holy and without blemish.
>
> Ephesians 5:25-27

God's vision for His house comprises two inseparable parts that are intimately related to each other: The first part deals with the entirety of the corporate body of believers and the second part describes what every individual member of the body of Christ should look like when our work is completed.

God's vision is that all people who believe in His Son should be one big body with no divisions.

> After this I beheld, and, lo, a great multitude, which no man could number, of all nations, and kindreds, and people, and tongues, stood before the throne, and before the Lamb, clothed with white robes, and palms in their hands...
> Revelation 7: 9-17

In eternity, God sees people from every nation and tribe and tongue gathered together. On earth today, He is looking to see the unity of the body. God sees neither division nor discrimination. He sees differences in physical characteristics, but not in the essence of being as the body of Christ. God does not see churches as being Black, White, Asian, African, or Caribbean, yet He sees people from all types of backgrounds belonging one to another, unified by His Son. God sees one big family living on earth. We are to draw strength from one another and live as one indestructible, indivisible body, bound by His love shed abroad in our hearts.

In many ways, the modern day Church seems to be nowhere near this picture. It has been said that if one wants to see the state of the Church, they should observe what happens on a Sunday morning. The Church is divided on racial, ethnic, and sometimes even economic lines. Needless to say, we must understand that God's vision has not changed. Whatever reason we assign to what is happening on earth today, God still sees His Church as undivided and non-segregated.

This book tells the story of how Bishop R. K. Hash and Mother Mildred Hash pastored a traditional small Black church and ordered their church according to the Word of God. When they embraced the principle of building the lives of people as their major thrust, it turned into a large multiracial, multiethnic community center. It was built on the Word of God and prayer. The congregation evolved into people of differing denominational backgrounds such as Catholic, Moravian, Methodist, Baptist, and many others. The congregation has learned how to appreciate each other's differences, thus making a harmonious body of believers striving for the faith of the gospel.

God's vision is that each individual should fully develop into the fullness of the character of His Son.

Here's the second part: God sees His people in the Church consists of individuals who have put on the full character of Christ, irrespective of their race, color, cultural or ethnic, or social or economic background. Jesus is described as the fullness of the expression of God. In Jesus, we see what God is like. Jesus is described as the Second Adam and in Him we see what we were made like before the fall.

God's vision calls for each one of us to eventually become like Him and regain what we lost due to the fall. We need God's nature to be able to dwell with Him forever in heaven. That is why we have the promise of being transformed at the sound of the last trumpet when God raptures the Church. Becoming like Christ is the ultimate goal for everyone who believes in Christ.

Today, we talk about weak Christians and strong Christians, but that is not God's idea. He sees everyone made whole in Christ. He sees every individual capable of fully representing the God-like character with which we were originally created.

> Till we all come in the unity of the faith, and of the knowledge of the Son of God, unto a perfect man, unto the measure of the stature of the fullness of Christ...
>
> Ephesians 4:13

God's vision is that through the Church, the earth will be filled with His Glory.

For the earth will be filled with the knowledge of the glory of the LORD, as the waters cover the sea.
                                                        Habakkuk 2:14

We commonly sing in our worship services, "Lord, we give you all the glory," but glory is not something we do nor is it something we give to God.

Glory is the by-product of what we look like and what we do. When our lives reflect all that God stands for such as holiness, power, abundance, and authority, then the earth is automatically filled with His glory. Men and women who look at us see something peculiar about us and are filled with awe. They see the beauty of holiness manifested in our lives, thereby filling the earth with God's glory. We don't "give" God glory by our words. Wherever that idea came from, it is wrong.

Glory is not something we do or handle. Glory is something that shows if it is present.

How do the heavens declare God's glory? We look at the sun, the moon, the stars, and all the planets in the universe and we exclaim, "This is beautiful!" Glory is the *reflection* of the life of God in the universe and in the saints on earth. Jesus said our lives should shine before men that we may glorify our heavenly Father who is in heaven; that is to fill the earth with God's glory.

The new phenomenon today is the mega church with its large congregations. The largest congregation is the one described in Revelation 7:14. Having a large congregation is not wrong. What is wrong is having a large congregation of people who are not exhibiting the character of Christ, people without love, and who refuse to change so God can use them as vessels through which He can manifest His glory, His reflection.

Implications for Church Leaders

God's vision is that the Church be a body of holy people of which every person is maturing in the things of God and understanding the mysteries of God. God's vision is that each person possesses the character of Christ. God's vision is that the Church live together as a family, drawing strength from each other, and living as one indestructible, indivisible body. God's vision is that, through the Church, the earth will be filled with the knowledge of the glory of the Lord. That is what God had in mind when He sent his Son to die on the cross. God's intent is to redeem the lost, whose lives are characterized by every kind of evil under the sun, and translate them into the kingdom of His Son where they will exhibit Christ-likeness.

Someone has made the remark that in America, progress is seen in terms of buildings, physical structures. We need physical structures, but striving to attain those things more than building lives come nowhere near God's idea of a church that is making progress. The large cathedrals, the multi-million dollar television studios, the jet for the pastor — none of these material signs of success come close to God's vision for the Church, no matter how hard we argue to justify them. As much as I believe that God has placed abundance here on earth for His family, when our aim to achieve these things supersedes the thrust to build people's lives, then certainly priorities are not properly aligned. Material things should be a true reflection of God's glory, not a manifestation of our own selfishness, false pride, contempt, ill-gotten gains, or misappropriation of God's money.

Every church leader should ask themselves the following questions:

1. How does God see my church?
2. What do members of my congregation look like when compared to the image of Jesus Christ our Lord?
3. Can God take at random any member of my congregation and see him or her as truly representing the image of His Son?
4. Are my members filled with the Holy Spirit, bearing the fruit of the Spirit, and being effective in Christian service?

5. What is the overall description of my church in terms of love, togetherness, and living as a family with no divisions?

These pivotal questions directly answer what is God's vision of the Church. These are the true parameters that God will use to evaluate the work we do as church leaders, whatever the capacity we find ourselves. Each one of us must therefore evaluate our vision again to see if it conforms to God's vision.

According to Acts 20:28, God wants every church leader to "take heed therefore unto yourselves, and to all the flock, over which the Holy Ghost hath made you overseers, to feed the church of God, which he hath purchased with his own blood."

The elders which are among you I exhort, who am also an elder, and a witness of the sufferings of Christ, and also a partaker of the glory that shall be revealed: *Feed the flock of God which is among you, taking the oversight thereof, not by constraint, but willingly; not for filthy lucre, but of a ready mind: Neither as being lords over God's heritage, but being ensamples to the flock.* And when the chief Shepherd shall appear, ye shall receive a crown of glory that fadeth not away.
I Peter 5: 1-4

So when they had dined, Jesus saith to Simon Peter, Simon, son of Jonas, lovest thou me more than these? He saith unto him, Yea, Lord; thou knowest that I love thee. He saith unto him, *Feed my lambs.* He saith to him again the second time, Simon, son of Jonas, lovest thou me? He saith unto him, Yea, Lord; thou knowest that I love thee. He saith unto him, *Feed my sheep.* He saith unto him the third time, Simon, son of Jonas, lovest thou me? Peter was grieved because he said unto him the third, Lovest thou me? And he said unto him, Lord, thou knowest all things; thou knoweth that I love thee. Jesus saith unto him, *Feed my sheep.*

John 21:15-17

Principles of Vision

For those who feel God is calling them into spiritual leadership, consider the following points regarding what you should perceive as your vision.

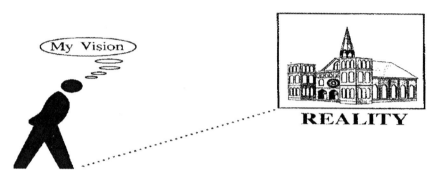

How can I achieve my vision? How can I get others to follow?

Write Your Vision

Pause for a moment. What is the specific purpose for the existence of your church or your ministry? Write an outline of your vision. This is your *word picture* of the finished product. It must be exciting to make people want to work to achieve it. It should be more than buildings and programs. It must be about how you plan to fulfill the vision of God to develop the lives of people.

> I will stand upon my watch, and set me upon the tower, and will watch to see what he will say unto me, and what I shall answer when I am reproved. And the LORD answered me, and said, *Write the vision, and make it plain upon tables,* that he may run that readeth it. For the vision is yet for an appointed time, but at the end it shall speak, and not lie: though it tarry, wait for it; because it will surely come, it will not tarry.
>
> Habakkuk 2:1-3

Make Your Vision Clear and Compelling

When you talk about your vision, light bulbs should go on! The clearer it is, the easier it will be to get people to volunteer their time, talents, and resources to make the vision a reality. Make sure that your vision inspires and motivates your members. Look at the following excerpt taken from Henry Ford's *Vivid Description – The Dream,* written in the 1920's when he built the first automobiles:

> "I will build a motor car for the great multitude...It will be so low in price that no man making a good salary will be unable to own one and enjoy with his family the blessing of hours of pleasure in God's great open spaces...When I'm through, everybody will be able to afford one, and everyone will have one. The horse will have disappeared from our highways; the automobile will be taken for granted... (and we will) give a large number of men employment at good wages."

Your vision must be stated such that it is compelling. It must burn in your heart or else it will not burn in the heart of your hearers.

A Vision is Timeless

The vision itself does not change. God did not change the vision He gave to Moses. The way in which the vision is carried out may change according to varying circumstances and situations, but the vision remains the same. Remember, God did not leave Israel in the wilderness. He provided a pillar of clouds to cool them by day, a fire to warm them at night, and manna to feed them each day. Although Moses did not see the promise land, God's plan to take the children of Israel from the bondage of Pharaoh remained the same.

I once heard a pastor teach that a generation is forty years. The children of Israel wandered for forty years, a whole generation, because Moses allowed other people's voices and opinions to go into his ear instead of locking on to the voice of God. Moses' weakness in delegating and developing leaders caused the vision that God placed in his hands to be carried out by the next generation. The blessing was for Moses, but he missed it because he listened to the murmuring of the people and became frustrated.

We see this happen many times in the body of Christ when a leader holds tight to his position as the senior pastor and is afraid to let the staff help him carry the burden; thus when the senior pastor passes from the scene, the church ends up in a split because no successor was trained to fill his shoes. I so admire Pastor Joel Osteen in Houston, Texas who tells the story of how he preaches in his father's shoes each Sunday. The late John Osteen and his son, Joel, are living examples of how the vision should never stop when one leader passes from the scene. If they have been trained well, the next leader will take the ministry to a greater level than the last.

- *A vision should involve and encompass* all the members of the church, the community, and the environment. It should be so big that if God isn't involved in it, it won't come to pass.

- *A vision should address all areas of needs.*
  Your vision should address the whole person as a triune being: spirit, soul, and body.

- *A vision should be time-specific.*
  This drives everyone towards a goal. It helps to establish milestones, or key success indicators, when the vision is cast. This way you can compare where you thought you would be and the environment you thought you would be in with reality. If there is a mismatch, you can go back and reexamine your objectives.

God's Vision in a Man's Heart
The Reuben K. & Mildred T. Hash Story

"Without vision, My people perish" Proverbs 29:18

Bishop R.K. Hash

Mother Mildred Hash

A Situation to Redeem

Living in the Piedmont Triad area of North Carolina, one will readily agree that churches are operating much better or differently than they did fifteen to twenty years ago. Now church music and order of services are more geared to meet the needs of this changing generation. Today's generation of worshippers are demanding more than rituals and traditions. They want a real relationship with their Creator and real answers to actual everyday challenges in their lives. Over the last 20 years or so, we've experienced a level of spiritual awakening in the Church that has broken traditions and denominational barriers that have dominated the Church for many years. This did not happen overnight though, because many old traditional practices were still being conducted in the Church.

Misinterpretation of the Scriptures

During the era of the '40s and '50s, many of the pastors and church leaders did not have the opportunity to go to school and did not really know how to read. As they stood to preach, they would have someone from the congregation, a reader, read the scriptures for them. Then the pastors would interpret the scriptures based upon their limited knowledge and then "hoop" to get the congregation shouting and screaming. After decades of this, the congregation expected to be emotionalized with hooping each time they came to church, but they were not being taught the Word of God, line upon line. As a result, church people depicted that of an impoverished, uneducated group of people swinging from the lights.

Misinterpretation of the scriptures caused church leaders to introduce extreme legalism that did not help people to grow. The churches restricted women from wearing certain things such as make-up, jewelry, and pants. Church members were not allowed to go to the movies or ballgames. Children were not even permitted to play games such as hopscotch or anything that appeared to be games of chance because it was considered to be gambling. Women, especially, were not allowed to be leaders in the church. Because they could only attend to the children or feed the poor, the women leaders were tagged with the title of either an evangelist or missionary.

Holding Up the Index Finger to Exit the Church

Have you ever attended a church service and saw someone hold up their index finger as they were exiting the sanctuary during the service? What does it mean? I was told that this tradition came about during slavery. When masters took their slaves with them to public gatherings, the slaves would always sit in the balcony. When the slave had to go to the bathroom or wanted to be excused for any other reason, they would hold their hand up and keep it up until their master acknowledged that they saw their hand and gave them permission to leave or, in other words, "excused them to leave". After the slave was given permission to leave, they would hold up one finger as they were leaving to inform anyone that saw them leave that they had been excused. So it means, "My Master has excused me." Holding up the index finger while leaving the sanctuary carried over into the Black church.

The Wearing of White Nets

Another traditional practice was that the women always wore a white net on their heads when they entered the church because it was equated as covering their glory. They took this belief from I Corinthians 11:15 which states, "But if a woman have long hair, it is a glory to her: for her hair is given her for a covering." As the years went by, the apostolic women began to wear fancy large hats and to this day, they are still known for their beautiful hats. My mother has over a hundred hats of all shapes, sizes, and colors. She has her hatboxes organized into her spring, summer, fall, and winter hats. It's a treat each Sunday to watch her as she enters the church.

The Wearing of Nurses Uniforms in the Church

In that era, women were the ushers of the church and they wore white nurses uniforms, complete with white caps, stockings, and shoes. When a person would get emotional under the spirit, or start foaming at the mouth, the nurses would run over with a box of tissues, gather around the person, and fan him or her until they calmed down.

Starting Services Late

The traditional Black Pentecostal church had a stigma of always starting their church services and events late. Most of the time their bulletins or printed materials were poorly printed and these things did not portray a ministry of excellence. They did not show the world the good, acceptable, and perfect will of God.

Bishop R. K. Hash, Sr.: An Agent of Change

These traditional practices showed the world that God runs an unorganized, thrown together, loose business. The administration, financial, and management order was unstructured, thus projecting a negative image of how the local church was packaged and presented to the world. What was needed then was a man who understood God's vision for the church and who would be used by

God to bring a drastic change in the state of affairs of the church. Things remained that way until God found His man, the person of the late Bishop R. K. Hash, Sr., and birthed in his heart the vision of change. My mom, Mother Mildred Hash, supported him as he launched the vision.

Although the eldest of fifteen children, born October 11, 1911, the late Bishop R. K. Hash, Sr. used life's challenges to learn all he could, because he knew that education was one of the major keys to achieving his dreams and fostering his successes. Farming was the major means of providing for families and the male children typically were required to stay at home to help the father with the farm. My dad's father, Mr. Jim Hash, however allowed him to go to school. Daddy had to walk two miles each way to get to and from "The Colored Children's School" as it was named. He completed the tenth grade, was awarded his diploma, and became qualified to become a teacher in "The Colored Children's School" in Woodlawn, VA.

Throughout his fifty years in ministry, Daddy was constantly taking correspondence courses and going to night classes to receive his B.S. degree in Metaphysical and Pastoral Counseling. He later received an honorary doctorate degree from Union Bible College in North Carolina. Education played a vital role in accomplishing what God called him to do.

The following paragraphs were taken from a short story that I wrote called, "Me and My Strong Black Mama."

These paragraphs briefly tell about the churches that Bishop and Mother Hash started before they moved to Winston Salem, North Carolina. Shortly after my dad and mom were married, they joined a "holiness" church, something that they thought they would never do. Mama used to laugh and make mockery of the holiness people because of the way that they danced and screamed in the church, but one day she found herself doing even worse.

To this date, at the beautiful age of eighty-four years old, Mother Hash tenaciously testifies of the fire shut up in her bones, and how she was filled with the Holy Ghost, and was once slain in the Spirit for three days. She was the first member of her family to get saved and for some unknown reason, I guess because they didn't understand what had happened to her, they rejected her because of the stand that she took for Christ. She still talks of that experience as if it happened yesterday.

Bishop and Mother Hash lived in a five room house in a coal mines camp in West Virginia and were very much in love and very happy. They had eleven children: Reuben, Jr., Mamie, Swanson, Joel, (twins) Delilah and Delores, Clyde, Charles, Leonard, Ronald, and finally me. The doctor told Mama that if she had another baby she would die. She said that in those days birth control information was not privy to Black people and that she and my daddy had tried all of the old wives tales methods of birth control that they knew.

Having another baby was surely not something that Mother Hash and Bishop planned, but there I was. When I was born, my mama died, but was revived through prayer. She said that she felt life leave her, but she also felt life come back into her. The doctor walked out of the room and said that he had done all that he could do. My daddy and a woman named Miss Francis Rose prayed for Mama and she came back. I became a little miracle child and my mama and daddy took me everywhere with them including church revivals throughout the country. I would boldly stand up on stage, wearing my pretty lacy dresses and socks, with a microphone in my hand and loudly sing the songs of the Lord. The congregation would shout and rejoice in the Lord under the anointing. I understand now why my parents were so protective of me. I thought they were just being strict. However, even as a child God had anointed me to minister to the body of Christ and they knew the importance of protecting the anointing.

When my dad's parents died, they took in his young brothers, Uncle Clyde, Uncle Marvin, Uncle George, and Uncle JY, until they were old enough to move out on their own. I'm not sure how it happened, but three of them married three sisters from their hometown area in Fries, Virginia, which is near the Grayson and Carroll counties. Each of them had very large families too, so I am blessed to have a lot of cousins who love the Lord and are singing, preaching, and serving God with all of their hearts. We are a tongue talking, singing, preaching, and shouting family. It's just in our blood. It's just who we are!

Building God's House

Moving from West Virginia to Virginia

When I was about three years old, my father moved us to a country town named Speedwell, Va., and started a church called High Point Holiness Church. We moved into a big two-story house that was deep in the country. My mama cried everyday because she had to leave her family and friends in West Virginia. This move connected Mama and Daddy to some life-long friends named the Boysaws, the Jacksons, the Jenkins, and the Peoples to name a few.

The nearest school for my older brothers and sisters to attend was about thirty minutes up the road in another small town named Wytheville, Va. There were no schools for Black children in Speedwell, so my brothers and sisters had to get up every morning at 4:00 AM to catch the 5:00 AM bus to travel to Wytheville. After about two years, Mama and Daddy moved our family to Wytheville. Once again we moved into a big white house, 460 East Washington Street, where Mama and Daddy started a church on the bottom floor.

The name of the church was Morning Star Church of God Apostolic. This little town did not have a holiness church and did not want one. Mama and Daddy received several anonymous bomb threats and letters. I remember we were in bed one night when we heard something loud hit the house. It was a firebomb. Daddy and Mama got everyone out of the house. I was so afraid, but like always, my strong mama made everyone feel safe.

Mama and Daddy devoted themselves to a lifelong service to humanity. They felt a divine urge to give to others and assumed the position of teachers and leaders to the hungering souls that came to be fed at the little country church they started. They always saw the good in people and strived to call forth the best qualities in everyone.

Daddy and Mama faithfully worked in the church teaching and singing and helping their members carry out their lives. They were diligent and faithful to the small things, which eventually led them into pastoring a very large ministry in their latter years. Everyone talked of what a great team they were preaching and singing. My mama's high-pitched melodious voice always stirred the audience to thunderous praise and shouting. In addition, my mama and daddy served on numerous community boards locally as well as nationally.

Mama and Daddy never ran from adversity. Adversity only

made them stronger. They had some families that supported their mission, namely the McKinneys, Mother Etta Mae Young, and Mother Emily Howard. They started having services in that little church that were so powerful that word soon got out all throughout the town and state about it. Mama would cook so much food as she entertained the traveling singing groups, The Royalaires, Don Degrate, The Silverlaires, The Mighty Clouds of Joy, and more. They entertained the bishops and elders, Bishop Smith, Bishop Odom, Bishop Pannell, Bishop Draft and their wives. The membership of the church grew and grew.

There were no Black schools in Galax, Austinville, and several other towns near Wytheville, so the Black kids from these towns had to catch the bus to Wytheville. Many of the young men who desired to play sports or to be in the school band had to find someone in Wytheville who would let them stay with them during the weekdays so they could stay after school to practice. Our home was a haven for many.

During the fifties and early sixties, when orphanages or hotels for African-Americans were uncommon, my mama's home became a refuge for many people.

Although Mama and Daddy's home was only a five-room haven, they still always made room to entertain preachers and to give a bed or some food to troubled kids, and sometimes to total strangers.

Daddy was the only Black minister who was a member of the local all White ministerial association in Wytheville. In those days, before we had the Black politicians that we are privileged to have today, the Black ministers were like politicians; they had a strong voice in the community as leaders. My mama's children were the first for many things in that small town. I was the first Black to work in the stores. I worked at the JJ Newberry's 5 & 10 Cents Store. My brother, Ronald, was the first Black professor at the local college. My brother, Joel, was the first Black security officer at the same local college.

Mama was the pastor of Little Zion Church of God Apostolic in a little country town called Fries, Va. On every first and third Sunday of the month, we would get up at 5:00 AM and I would drive her to Fries. The people there had so much love for my mama. They would have big homecoming services and people from everywhere would come. The ladies of the church would cook and they seemed to have enough food to serve an army. Her little congregation, to name a few, consisted of Bessie and Jessie Jenkins, Mae Anderson, and Deacon and Mother Hurd Johnson. One Sunday during service, Deacon Johnson fainted and died. This was such a sad day, because Deacon Johnson was one of the original founders and a devout pillar of the church. My brother, Leonard, later became the pastor. Leonard is now recovering from a muscular illness, but the church is still going strong today with a new pastor.

While I was living in Detroit, my mama and daddy moved to Winston Salem, NC to pastor a church named St. Peter's Church of God Apostolic. They also adopted a five-month-old baby boy named John Christopher—baby number twelve. They purchased a beautiful house, but the closets weren't large enough for my mama's clothes, shoes, and hats, so Daddy built another room just for her. You see, my mama did without so much when she was raising the family that my daddy later spoiled her and showered her with about anything she wanted.

The Call and Vision

Bishop Hash so vividly told the story of how, in 1940, the Lord opened his eyes to see the state of the churches throughout the country and, in particular, the Church of God Apostolic organization. He knew that there was a need to break what had become traditions that kept God's people from growing spiritually, thus affecting their total life. Bishop Hash's experience was similar to what happened to two servants of God whose account is recorded in the Scriptures, namely Moses and Nehemiah. Here's an account of Moses' experience with God.

> And the LORD said, I have surely seen the affliction of my people which are in Egypt, and have heard their cry by

reason of their taskmasters; for I know their sorrows; And I am come down to deliver them out of the hand of the Egyptians, and to bring them up out of that land unto a good land and a large, unto a land flowing with milk and honey; unto the place of the Canaanites, and the Hittites, and the Amorites, and the Perizzites, and the Hivites, and the Jebusites. Now therefore, behold, the cry of the children of Israel is come unto me: and I have also seen the oppression wherewith the Egyptians oppress them. *Come now therefore, and I will send thee unto Pharaoh, that thou mayest bring forth my people the children of Israel out of Egypt.*
Exodus 3:7-10

God gave Moses a vivid picture of what was happening to the children of Israel in Egypt. He needed to see the exact situation God was calling him to as well as a picture of what God wanted to do. You always have those two components in a vision that comes from God. Moses had a blueprint of God's vision for His people. He was to take God's people from Egypt into the promised land. At the time God spoke with Moses on the mountain, God saw the Israelites settled in the land of Canaan.

Does anyone remember what happened to Nehemiah when he heard about the state of Jerusalem as he served in the king's palace in Susa? What did God ask Nehemiah to do? We can infer God's desires from the request He made to the king.

The words of Nehemiah the son of Hachaliah. And it came to pass in the month Chisleu, in the twentieth year, as I was in Shushan the palace, That Hanani, one of my brethren, came, he and certain men of Judah; and I asked them concerning the Jews that had escaped, which were left of the captivity, and concerning Jerusalem. And they said unto me, The remnant that are left of the captivity there in the province are in great affliction and reproach: the wall of Jerusalem also is broken down, and the gates thereof are burned with fire.
Nehemiah 1:1-3

And it came to pass in the month Nisan, in the twentieth year of Artaxerxes the king, that wine was before him: and I took up the wine, and gave it unto the king. Now I had not been beforetime sad in his presence. Wherefore the king said unto me, Why is thy countenance sad, seeing thou art not sick? this is nothing else but sorrow of heart. Then I was very sore afraid, And said unto the king, Let the king live for ever: why should not my countenance be sad, when the city, the place of my fathers' sepulchres, lieth waste, and the gates thereof are consumed with fire? Then the king said unto me, For what dost thou make request? So I prayed to the God of heaven.

Nehemiah 2:1-4

Nehemiah saw in his mind's eye a city rebuilt, the worship of God restored, and the affliction of the people reversed. That explains the request for wood and other materials that Nehemiah made to the king. His vision was to see a Jerusalem rebuilt with its people living in happiness and prosperity, and with the temple worship fully restored.

What did Bishop Hash see when God spoke to him?

1. A church where every member is knowledgeable in the Word of God rather than in the traditions of men.
2. A gap between the church and the community that needed to be bridged. His vision of the church was a center that reaches out into the community, providing healing to the hurting, delivering the oppressed; a church that is not confined to itself but reaching out to bring life and healing to its immediate community and beyond.
3. A breaking down of the congregational boundaries that keeps one church insulated from the other, but living and working together in unity with one another throughout the Triad.
4. A church that is drawing from all the resources God has placed in the entire body of Christ and not just one denomination or congregation.

Bishop Hash wanted the work he started to continue even after he was gone by people in whose hearts remain the things that God had called him to do. He often told the story of a vision that he had while sitting in the pulpit of the church, in which he saw a large field of beautiful flowers and down in the flowers were thousands of babies. The Lord confirmed to him that this meant that the work He had called him to do was so large it would take a lot of young people with much energy to bring it to pass. When he saw the state of the youth in the Triad area, he knew something had to be done to change their future and destiny. Many of them did not have confidence to believe they could achieve a college education or own a home. Some had never traveled out of Winston Salem or had taken a vacation. These trends had existed from one generation to the next.

Bishop R.K. Hash, Sr. and Mother Mildred Hash distinctly heard the vision of God for His church. They devoted their lives wholeheartedly to the scriptures for directives to run God's corporation on earth, His Church. To do this, the Lord commanded Bishop Hash to teach neither about man's denominations, nor traditions, but only about God and His Word, line upon line and precept upon precept.

Bishop and Mother Hash, like all other leaders, had the task to execute the vision God had given them the best way they could. Bishop Hash adopted biblical principles of how to grow a church and brought great revival to the churches in the Triad area. Many people initially made mockery of Bishop Hash and his wife, some sending anonymous threatening letters and bomb threats simply because of their stand to break traditions that had been set in the church, such as how to dress and where to allow people to go. Bishop and Mother Hash, however, demonstrated cheerful spirit-filled hearts that were full of joy and happiness, and were eventually loved by not only their flock, but by the entire community and people worldwide. Everyone knows them as Dad and Mother Hash. They left a legacy for the body of Christ that lives on up to the present.

The words, pioneer, impact, and legacy best describe the life and work of Mother Mildred Hash and the late Bishop R. K. Hash, Sr. They provided a legacy for the twenty-first century Church to follow. It may not ever be known just how much the vision that God placed in their hearts and their firm stand of righteousness have impacted churches and leaders in that part of the U.S., and eventually throughout the world.

True Shepherds

Bishop and Mother Hash were true shepherds. Unger's Bible Dictionary defines the word shepherd as "to tend" or "one who tends". It goes on to say that he leads his flock from the fold, going before them, calling them, and finding those who stray. He supplies them with water, and finally he watches their entrance by night. Bishop and Mother Hash performed these actions in an exemplary manner as the pastors of their church flock. Without fail, they labored tirelessly to teach and preach the Word of God nourishing their flock with rich spiritual food for growth and living.

True Servants

Mark 10:45 says, "For even the son of man did not come to be served, but to serve and give His life a ransom for many." These qualities were evident in both Bishop and Mother Hash. They *gave* of themselves for their flock's good and often put their flock's needs before their own. Many times, they also gave their finances to the church or to those in need. This is the unselfish spirit that they displayed daily to their congregation.

Great Visionaries

Bishop and Mother Hash were great visionaries of wisdom who had a direct mission to accomplish during their lifetime on earth. Anyone who has known them from far and near knew them to be the epitome of integrity. They were known to be upright, fair, and rock solid in their principles and beliefs in God.

As this book develops, we will explore how Bishop Hash practically applied biblical principles of growing a church to make his vision come through.

Mother Hash: Partner in the Vision

If there ever was a Proverb woman, Mother Hash is the epitome of one. My mother did not have an opportunity to get a formal education. In fact, she did not get past the third grade, because being the oldest child, she had to help her mother take care of her eleven brothers and sisters. Then she got married at 15 years old and had eleven children of her own to raise. This was typical in that era. There was a lady named Miss Gholson who begged my grandmother to let Mama go to school, but she would not let her go. This did not stop Mama. She decided to teach herself. Mother Hash has a wisdom about her that is unexplainable, yet profound. She still speaks at conferences, provides counsel to people from all over the country, and today everyone knows her to be a woman of much wisdom. Her education came from life experiences and the favor of God as she worked alongside my father and supported him in the ministry.

All throughout my childhood, my mother kept our house full of book series such as Little Black Sambo, the Bobsy Twins, and more. We did not have a television in our home until I was fourteen years old, so when we got home from school, our first chore was to sit at the kitchen table and do homework. Mama loved her family so much that her mother accused her of loving us too much. Today, Mama Hash, as she is affectionately known throughout the country, travels to speak to pastor's wives of the twenty-first century instructing them how to be the support that is needed by their great men of God, their husbands.

Mother Hash, at fifty-seven years old, had never driven a car before but took driving lessons and then bought herself a car with a hatchback. She peddled home decorations to raise money for the church building fund. She started an auxiliary called the Willing Workers and they did every project they could think of to raise money for the building fund.

She is still strong in health and travels throughout the country speaking at conferences and giving consultation to pastor's wives. Mother Hash is still shouting, singing, and preaching with the fire of a sixteen-year-old.

Bishop R. K. and Mother Hash were married for fifty-seven years and raised 12 children. To date, 45 grandchildren, 26 great grandchildren, and 12 great-great grand children can be accredited to their union. All of their sons and daughters are pastors, administrators, or fulfilling active ministries in the body of Christ.

The Visit to Tulsa, Oklahoma

At the age of sixty-nine, Bishop and Mother Hash went to Tulsa, Oklahoma to visit their son, Elder J. C. Hash, Sr. and his family who were attending Rhema Bible Institute. One day while sitting in a class under the teaching of Kenneth Hagin, Sr., the Lord reminded him of the vision that He had put in his heart and what He had instructed him to do forty years ago. He heard these words, "Who is stopping you now?"

This was a pivotal season in the life of Bishop and Mother Hash as they returned from Tulsa with renewed energy and inspiration. They heeded to the call to stand firm on what God had told them to do. There was a bright continence on Bishop Hash's face; probably like that of Moses when he came off the mountain after spending three days hearing from God about how to lead the children of Israel out of Egypt to the promise land. His beautiful thick white hair shined like a halo and he testified of how God had renewed his energy like that of a young man. Bishop Hash had banners made that read "Growth is impossible without change; cope with it so we can grow stronger together." He had the banners sent to all of the churches in the Church of God Apostolic organization throughout the country.

> **Growth Is Impossible Without Change**
> **...Cope with it so we can grow stronger together.**

What To Do With the Vision of God in Your Heart

1. Create awareness in the hearts and minds of your people about what God wants to do with them through sharing the vision.
2. Organize yourself to create the order needed to carry out the vision.
3. Devise a strategy to care for and develop people, because this is the heartbeat of God in his vision.

4. Find ways to globalize the vision, because it goes beyond your congregation.
5. Put in place a conscious plan to raise a successor to the vision.

God has placed great men and women on the earth who are professional strategists, marketers, and business planners. All of the answers to achieve the vision of God are in His Word.

All scripture is given by inspiration of God, and is profitable for doctrine, for reproof, for correction, for instruction in righteousness: That the man of God may be perfect, thoroughly furnished unto all good works.
II Timothy 3:16-17

Corporate trainers such as Stephen Covey, Peter Lowe, Tom Peter's, Zig Zigler, Les Brown, and others have been placed on this earth to embrace corporations and their visions with proven strategies, statistics, and concepts for the twenty-first century. The Church must understand that the same business strategies that cause phenomenal growth for corporate 500 companies will also work for the corporate Church. The Church is a business. The only difference is that our business is building the lives of people. If you listen to the teaching concepts that they use to make multi-million-dollar businesses successful, they are all principles that have been taken from the Word of God. Customer service is nothing but treating others as you would want others to treat you. Stephen Covey's *Seven Steps of Highly Effective People* can equate to the principles outlined in Psalms 37:1-8 in the Holy Bible, as follows:

Step One: *Fret not thyself because of evildoers, neither be thou envious against the workers of iniquity. For they shall soon be cut down like the grass, and wither as the green herb.*
Step Two: *Trust in the Lord, and do good (study to do the smart thing, the honest thing): so shalt thou dwell in the*

land *(You'll be able to sit amongst business investors), and verily thou shalt be fed (have favor).*
Step Three: *Delight thyself also in the Lord; and he shall give thee the desires of thine heart.*
Step Four: *Commit thy way unto the Lord, trust also in him; and he shall bring it to pass. And he shall bring forth thy righteousness as the light, and thy judgment as the noonday.*
Step Five: *Rest in the Lord, (Don't worry, be happy) and wait patiently for him: fret not thyself because of him who prospereth in his way, because of the man who bringeth wicked devices to pass.*
Step Six: *Cease from anger. Stay calm. Study and know your business.*
Step Seven: *Forsake wrath: fret not thyself in any wise to do evil. For evildoers shall be cut off: but those that wait upon the Lord, they shall inherit the earth.*

I am a Christian consultant, motivational speaker, and administrator that specialize in ministry operations to help pastors fulfill their visions. This is who I am. This is what I do and what I know. Corporations know the value of hiring experts, because their bottom line is always profit at any cost, whereas the bottom line of the Church is to win souls at any cost. There is no excuse for ignorance today and it is OK to say I don't know or I can't do everything. It's OK, it's OK, it's OK pastors for you not to know how to do everything. The wisest pastors are the ones who surround themselves with people who are stronger than they are in specific skills. Be sure to:

- staff your weaknesses and
- build your inner circle.

When you have order and structure, souls are saved, lives are changed, and the kingdom of God is steadily increasing. No one can put a price tag on this invaluable gift. God called Aaron to be Moses' chief administrator.

He was the first appointed high priest of the Hebrew nation.

- God designated him to be Moses' official spokesperson.
- He received instructions from God for observing the first Passover.
- In the wilderness, he assisted Moses in keeping order and rendering judgment over the people.
- Both he and Moses were singled out when the people complained about the harsh conditions of the wilderness.
- God gave special instructions about the robe that he would wear to signify his status in the priesthood.
- The tabernacle, which was the main place of worship, was under Aaron's supervision.
- God gave him instructions concerning the functions of the priesthood and the tabernacle.
- He alone, serving in the capacity of high priest, went into the Holy of Holies on the Day of Atonement.

The bottom line is that Aaron, Moses' chief administrator, was responsible for the order and spiritual leadership of the Hebrew nation. He established guidelines and processes to institute the commands that God gave to Moses. Moses was God's direct representative, but Aaron was his mouthpiece and interpreter to the people. Moses carried the "what" and Aaron carried the "how." Selah. Think on this.

CHAPTER TWO

Strategy Two

Build People:
The Heartbeat of God's Vision

"If you love Me, feed my sheep"

Place the People at the Center of the Vision

The greatest prayer one can pray for someone entering into full-time ministry or any position of spiritual leadership is that they will *grasp just an inkling of the importance God places on people.* This is the point most people miss in Christian leadership. The message conveyed today is that when people pray, "Lord, I want to be used by You," it has more to do with having their names high up there on the stock market. Any time a minister of the gospel becomes more interested in keeping his or her name up in lights than to what happens to the flock of God, it is obvious that they have been sidetracked and have missed the point of their call.

Godly principles, used to mold and develop God's people, should be in the limelight. As a result of these principles, God will make your name great.

Many pastors have this turned around and are seeking fame for themselves and then place the blame on their leaders when it doesn't happen for them. They go away to large conferences and return to their staff frustrated and wondering why they aren't producing the same results; thus they set an atmosphere of frustration and discouragement among their staff. Because they have not taken the time to have a professional master plan with timelines, equipment, technology, and budgets, they will never achieve the same results that they have seen at big conferences. These pastors don't even realize that their lack of leadership and administrative skills is the problem. Because of this, there is a very a high turnover of leaders and staff in every church.

Building people is the very essence of every Bible-based ministry. When we begin taking people for granted, and exploiting them for their kind hearts, talents, and money, we can consider our ministry ended. The rest is just doing something to please us, because it certainly does not please God.

The truth about the importance God places on people is a theme that runs throughout the entire Bible.

Broken People:
The Church is like the trauma center of a hospital.

Many people do not seek God until the pressures of life have broken them down. No matter what people in the pews may look like or how much money they may have in the bank, many of them have broken hearts. Every one of them has a story. Some have lost their jobs, their homes, have gone through divorces, illness, lost children, addicted to drugs and alcohol, and the list could go on and on. But the fact is, everyone has a story.

Some of the brokenness comes from generational curses in the same way that certain physical illnesses, such as high blood pressure and diabetes, are hereditary. And emotional illnesses can be inherited too.

- Have you ever wondered why it is so difficult to work with church people?
- Why is there always so much tension in the church?
- Why does it take so long to get projects done?
- Why is it that most church people have little finances?
- Why do so many church people have emotional instability and low self-esteem?

Many church members are broken people who smile on the outside but are miserable on the inside. The memories of hurt and pain may be stored in their subconscious and they aren't even aware why they are moody, short fused, shy, easily intimidated, or can't seem to break bad habits.

Broken people come to the emergency room looking for some medicine or something to ease the pain. They want something to put their lives back together. They may spend hours and hours sitting in the emergency waiting room at the hospital. And even when they finally see the doctor, the medicine prescribed may or may not cure the illness or bring immediate relief. The healing process may take weeks, months, and even years.

If church people don't get immediate results, then they run to another church, and another church, and another seeking satisfaction. If singing and shouting and loud preaching were the only antidotes to heal, then most of our churches would be full of healed people. However, you and I know that this is not the case.

I believe Hosea 4:6 is one of the most powerful scriptures in the Bible, because *until our church structure is organized to meet the needs of the whole person, and to teach people about themselves as a whole person, we will continue to just have church as usual.* People will come to church, sing and shout, listen to the sermon, and go back home with the same problems, fears, hurt, and pain that they have always carried. This will go on from generation to generation.

God called my brother, Dr. Ronald Hash, to a small town with a population of only about 2,000 people. The town is very heavily plagued with drugs, incest, and social problems that the average pastor would not even touch. His church sits right smack down in the heart of it. Growing up, Ronald was always very studious and achieved many honors. He was a dean at a major university, owned a very large business, and appeared to really be on top of this game called life. But one day, God told him to pack up everything and move his family to Tulsa, Oklahoma to attend Rhema Bible Institute. My brother, J.C., my sister, Delilah, and several of my family members have all graduated from Rhema, but it was especially remarkable when Dr. Ronald Hash, the professor, announced that he too was packing up and going there.

I was privy to spend a couple of months with him and his family as I was finishing this book. One day we were walking down the street from the church to look at four houses that he wanted to purchase to use as homes for abused women with children. He already has two large houses for homeless veterans and a training center where they receive assistance in their recovery that helps usher them back into productive and successful living, thus connecting them back with their families.

As we were walking to the houses, four little girls ranging in ages about five to twelve were playing in the grass. All of a sudden, a black car stopped with four women in it and one of the women yelled out of the window at the smallest girl. She said, "What the h_ _ _ are you doing out here? I told your little a_ _ not to come out of the house! I'm going to beat your a_ _ if you don't get back in that d_ _ _ house now!" Then she and the women in the car drove off and just left the girls. It didn't seem to affect the girls at all because they continued to play. One of the little girls spoke to me and said, "Are you going to give me some money?"

What I saw was a situation where these girls have become numb at hearing this type of verbal abuse and it didn't seem to affect them at all. They evidently have seen their mothers getting money from total strangers, so they think that it is appropriate behavior to ask strangers for money too. They will grow up and think that it's OK for men to talk to them the same way that their mothers talked to them as they were growing up.

The point that I'm making here is that this is a generational curse. It will go on and on if the church does not change this direction of their lives through strategic teaching and relationship building with their communities.

I have been so amazed at how my brother and his wife have embraced their Church community with so much love. It's hard to believe that anyone could have enough love to deal with these types of situations on a daily basis.

Here's another story about my brother, Dr. Ron: One Sunday night, about 10:00 PM, he received a call from the hospital concerning an elderly lady from his church neighborhood who had fallen and was taken to the emergency room. There was no family member for them to contact. My brother and I immediately got in the car and drove to the hospital. When we arrived, they had placed her in a room away from everyone else. Her body and clothes reeked with a horrendous odor. Her hair, teeth, and nails were very dirty.

This didn't stop Dr. Ron at all. Although he called some of the other ladies of the church to come to her assistance, he took his time to drive all around town to help the old lady try to find her nephew. We had to ride with all of the windows down, but we eventually found the nephew and placed her in his care.

When God called Moses in Mount Horeb, it was not about Moses. It was about the children of Israel.

God said to Moses, "I have seen the affliction of My people in Egypt...." Those were God's opening remarks. Does that send a message? Moses did not set foot on the promised land because He did not honor God before the people. God's focus in the miracles He did was on the people and not to show Moses as a man of power.

Again, here's God expressing through the prophet Ezekiel His disgust with the shepherds of Israel who missed the whole point of their leadership and authority:

> And the word of the LORD came unto me, saying, Son of man, prophesy against the shepherds of Israel, prophesy, and say unto them, Thus saith the Lord GOD unto the shepherds; *Woe be to the shepherds of Israel that do feed themselves! should not the shepherds feed the flocks?* Ye eat the fat, and ye clothe you with the wool, ye kill them that are

fed: but ye feed not the flock. The diseased have ye not strengthened, neither have ye healed that which was sick, neither have ye bound up that which was broken, neither have ye brought again that which was driven away, neither have ye sought that which was lost; but with force and with cruelty have ye ruled them. And they were scattered, because there is no shepherd: and they became meat to all the beasts of the field, when they were scattered. My sheep wandered through all the mountains, and upon every high hill: yea, my flock was scattered upon all the face of the earth, and none did search or seek after them.

Ezekiel 34:1-6

It is wise for anyone called into the position of spiritual leadership to evaluate him or herself against this statement God made, because somewhere, some day, this passage will come up and you better be ready to give a good response to God! Continue reading the rest of this chapter to see what God will do to the shepherds.

A good study of the "woes" recorded in the Bible shows how many of them are related to God's displeasure at people having been maltreated. When God declares "woe," it is not to be taken for granted. It means God is angry about whatever it was that made Him make such a declaration. God has not changed that position; therefore, we cannot set our own standards. We have to minister to His people by His standards of love, integrity, and compassion. Anything else is not acceptable.

Jesus warned us about what happens to anyone who causes any of the little ones to stumble. Read this for yourself:

Take heed that ye despise not one of these little ones; for I say unto you, That in heaven their angels do always behold the face of my Father which is in heaven. For the Son of man is come to save that which was lost. How think ye? if a man have an hundred sheep, and one of them be gone astray, doth he not leave the ninety and nine, and goeth into the mountains, and seeketh that which is gone astray? And if so be that he find it, verily I say unto you, he rejoiceth more of that sheep, than of the ninety and nine which went not astray. Even so it is not the will of your Father which is in heaven, that one of these little ones should perish.

Matthew 18:10-14

Woe unto you, scribes and Pharisees, hypocrites! for ye compass sea and land to make one proselyte, and when he is made, ye make him twofold more the child of hell than yourselves.

Matthew 23:15

But whoso shall offend one of these little ones which believe in me, it were better for him that a millstone were hanged about his neck, and that he were drowned in the depth of the sea.

Matthew 18:6

When the disciples wanted to command fire to consume the Samaritans, Jesus told them the Son of God came to save men, not to destroy them. If you are reading this book, the chances are that you have seen or heard of the movie, *The Passion of the Christ*.

The question to ask is this: Why did Jesus have to endure all the pain and shame if He had the power to prevent it or stop it at anytime?

The answer is simple: People! People! People!

Jesus loves people!

For most people, getting into the ministry is synonymous with an ability to preach and to explain what is in the Bible. However, they do not consider the long-term investment of continual time, energy, resources, prayer, fasting, and studying the Word that is necessary to effectively minister to people. My mother made the following profound statement regarding this issue:

> "Many young pastors of this generation are going into the ministry for fame and fortune and do not have the calling to minister to people on every level. They only have a heart for the rich and well-to-do, but when it comes to reaching down and putting their arms around a homeless man or woman, they would never do it."

If you don't have that same weight of burden that propelled Jesus to go through hardship, then re-examine your excitement about becoming a pastor. Otherwise, you're in the business for the wrong reason.

Jumping onto the spiritual leadership bandwagon is a more serious task than most people realize. Let us all be careful to understand what we mean when we tell people, "I feel the Lord is calling me into full-time ministry."

Teach the People God's Word

The importance of God's Word in building people cannot be overemphasized. God's Word is the first tool the church leader has in the building process. Today, churches are using all kinds of means to get people to come to church, especially young people. Most people fail to teach the unadulterated Word of God and thus the common complaint you hear from preachers about church members is that they are not living the life of Christ.

One of the primary charges God gave Bishop Hash was to teach His Word. Everyone knows that Apostolic preachers preach with the thunder and vigor of God and can usually sing, shout, wipe sweat, and hoop all at the same time. They can have the congregation shouting and throwing handkerchiefs and falling out on the floor when they preach. This was typical for Bishop Hash, too, but when he returned from Tulsa where the Lord had revisited him while sitting in a Kenneth Hagin, Sr.'s class, he settled his sermon down and became a teaching preacher. He heavily taught this manner of teaching to the other associate pastors as well, because they were following the hooping tradition of the Apostolic pastors.

I probably need to make it crystal clear right here that I still love to hear some hoop sometimes, but I know that I cannot live off of hoop alone. We must hear God's Word with our spirit, not our emotions and intellect. Two times the Bible tells us the importance of really hearing the word:

> But he answered and said, It is written, Man shall not live by bread alone, but by every word that proceedeth out of the mouth of God.
>
> Matthew 4:4

> And Jesus answered him, saying, It is written, That man shall not live by bread alone, but by every Word of God.
>
> Luke 4:4

Abel, Enoch, Noah, Abraham, Sara, Isaac, Jacob, Joseph, and Moses are our examples of faith in God's Word.

> Now faith *[in God's word]* is the substance of things hoped for, the evidence of things not seen. For by it the elders obtained a good report (success, healing, fullness). Through faith we understand that the worlds were framed *by the word of God,* so that things which are seen were not made of things which do appear.

- By faith *[in God's word]* Abel offered unto God a more excellent sacrifice than Cain, by which he obtained witness that he was righteous. (v.4)
- By faith *[in God's word]* Enoch was translated that he should not see death; and was not found, because God had translated him: for before his translation he had this testimony, that he pleased God. (v.5)
- By faith *[in God's word]* Noah, being warned of God of things not seen as yet, moved with fear, prepared an ark to the saving of his house: by the which he condemned the world, and became heir of the righteousness which is by faith. (v.7)

- By faith *[in God's word]* Abraham, when he was called to go out into a place which he should after receive for an inheritance, obeyed; and he went out, not knowing whither he went. (v.8)
- Through faith *[in God's word]* Sara herself received strength to conceive seed, and was delivered of a child when she was past age, because she judged him faithful who had promised. (v. 11)
- By faith *[in God's word]* Abraham, when he was tried, offered up Isaac: and he that had received the promises offered up his only begotten son. (v.17)
- By faith *[in God's word]* Isaac blessed Jacob and Esau concerning things to come. (v.20)
- By faith *[in God's word]* Jacob when he was a dying, blessed both the sons of Joseph; and worshipped, leaning upon the top of his staff. (v.21)
- By faith *[in God's word]* Joseph, when he died, made mention of the departing of the children of Israel; and gave commandment concerning his bones. (v.22)
- By faith *[in God's word]* Moses, when he was come to years, refused to be called the son of Pharaoh's daughter; Choosing rather to suffer affliction with the people of God, than to enjoy the pleasures of sin for a season. (vv.24-25)

Hebrews 11:1-25

A School of Ministry to Replace the Traditional Sunday School Hour

Bishop Hash instituted a School of Ministry that replaced the traditional Sunday school hour. When you ask the average person from most any religion to explain what they believe and why, they can fluently articulate their belief. However, when you ask the average Christian what they believe and why, they hesitate. If we truly believe that God is supreme and that we believe that Jesus lived and died on the cross for our sins and the sins of the world, then we too should be able to articulate with clarity the reasons for our belief. Hosea 4:6 explicitly tells us that we do not succeed because of lack of knowledge.

The School of Ministry consisted of classes for the entire family that were taught basic biblical principles. The deacons and ministers of the church taught the classes not only to spread out the workload, but to give them the opportunity to use their teaching gifts as well. Bishop Hash taught a lot on topics such as salvation, the infilling of the Holy Spirit, the importance of speaking in tongues, the blood covenant, baptism, spiritual gifts, church government, and leadership to name a few.

The School of Ministry topics are as follows:

Membership Foundation Class
 1. You Must Be Born Again
 2. You are the Righteousness of God
 3. Your Faith Has Made You Whole
 4. Healing for Christians
 5. Baptism of the Holy Spirit
 6. Victorious Abundant Life
 7. Confessing God's Word
 8. Developing the Human Spirit
 9. Tithes and Offerings
 10. Vision of the Ministry
 11. The Helps Ministry
 12. Fasting

Ministry of Helps Class
 1. Supportive Ministries
 2. Jesus and the Ministry of Helps
 3. Called, Appointed, and Anointed
 4. Doubling Your Ability through God
 5. Sensitivity of Heart
 6. Helps Ministry Guidelines and Procedures
 7. Helps Workers Training Guide
 8. Decently and in Order
 9. How to Relate to Your Pastor
 10. The Attitude of a Servant
 11. Leadership Share-in
 12. Video – God Uses Stars and Candles

Ambassador/Leadership Training Class
1. Introduction – Proper Attitudes Towards Leadership
2. Touch Not Mine Anointed
3. Are You in the Right Church?
4. God's Attitudes
5. Know Your Leadership
6. Submission
7. Support – Financial, Prayer, Physical
8. Video #1 – Faithfulness, the Crowbar of God
9. Video #2 – Faithfulness, the Crowbar of God
10. Managing Different Work Styles
11. Time Management Part I
12. Time Management Part II
    The Authority of God – Spiritual and Delegated:

Spiritual Authority
1. Introduction to Authority
2. God – The Supreme Authority
3. The Authority of Believers
4. Exercising Authority
5. Rebellion – A Satanic Principle
6. The Manifestations of Man's Rebellion
7. Authority – Not Might, Not Power, But Spirit

Delegated Authority
1. Delegated Authority – God's Choice
2. The Basis for Being in Delegated Authority
3. Misuse of Authority – Preventive Maintenance
4. Clean, Holy, Set Apart – Your Ultimate Challenge
5. Delegated Authority – Attitude of the Heart

The curriculum for the topics were selected from books from the church bookstore. This strategy provoked a habit for the members to read, study, and build their personal library with the Word of God.

Understanding the Purpose of Ministry

Bishop Hash's teachings on Sundays, at the Wednesday Bible study services, and across the board, brought understanding of the purpose for ministry operations and many began to see themselves as gifts to the body of Christ. Even though the promises of God are "yea and amen," we first must know how to use the manual, the Bible, which God left us.

Many times when people first come to Christ, they do not get involved in the ministry for many reasons. Many people have a low self-esteem and do not think they are important enough to do the work of a holy God. Some did not get the opportunity to go to college and thus they don't think they are smart enough. Some think that they were so bad before they got saved that they will never be good enough to do God's work. Some people's lives were so bad that they didn't want to go to hell if they died, and so they had nowhere else to turn but to the Church.

No matter what the reasons were for people coming to the Church, their lives became a reflection of the glory of God as they began to understand God's vision and strategy for raising a healthy church. They learned the fact that God uses people who are willing to yield to His Word to become living epistles, regardless of their education, economic status, or background.

The Principles of Giving

Another important principle Bishop Hash taught was the principle of giving. People were taught how to apply the Word of God to their tithes and offerings, and were taught to understand that their giving was a reflection of their direct relationship with God. They no longer begged for offerings. They no longer felt coerced to give.

This move erased the spirit of poverty that many times hovers over the people in the pews. The world judges success by material things; the human faculties of sight, sound, taste, touch, and smell move them. The people were empowered to live the life that God promised them by educating them in both natural and supernatural concepts and principles.

I need to emphasize at this point the difference between giving tithes and offerings versus giving a sacrifice. I believe we all agree with Malachi 3:10 that instructs us to bring our tithes to the house of God, but when a sacrificial offering has been held in the church, over the years I've watched people give money that is not theirs to give. Mark 12:17 and Luke 20:25 both instruct us to render unto Caesar the things which are Caesar's, and unto God the things which are God's. In other words, after you have brought the holy tithes and offering to God's house, if you have not paid your landlord, your mortgage, utility bills and other creditors, you don't have anything else to give. The Bible demands that we pay our bills.

Now, if you want to make a sacrifice, use any monies that you allocate in your budget for recreation or other luxuries such as hair, nails, clothes, etc. I know that this is not always taught in most churches, but it is the truth. This practice is another reason that many churches have painted a picture of an impoverished people to the world. We must pay our bills on time. This issue must be addressed strongly in the local churches to turn the picture around of how the world sees the Church. Not to mention that our children are watching us.

Giving Spiritual Gifts to God

Your congregation must be taught how to look within themselves and to understand the gifts that God places inside everyone. Many people have turned those gifts into professions and businesses. Start classes to teach solid business techniques and you will see an entrepreneurial spirit saturate your congregation. Practically everyone will have either a home business or will testify of going to real estate school and so on. Watch how this will impact your offerings.

One of the stories that I love to tell is about a lady named Mother Effie. The gift that she gives back to God is to make sure the glasses for the pulpit water are always sparkling. She keeps the silver goblets clean, sets up the oil and water at the altar for baby dedications, places a white cloth and oil for the healing line, and crisply irons a white handkerchief for Bishop Hash. She takes so much pride in her contribution to the body of Christ that she has looked up every scripture in the Bible about serving water and its' meaning, and has written an operations manual. She even keeps a log of the favorite types of drinks of all the guest speakers that visited the church. Her devout dedication to her spiritual gift of serving water has developed such a reputation that pastors regularly ask her to come to their churches to train their staff.

Mother Effie started a silver and brass cleaning business and had some business cards made. Her gift made room for her. God rewards diligence. At approximately sixty-five years of age, she bought herself a car, travels, dresses sharply all of the time, and does whatever she wants to do.

The same Lord and the same Spirit placed all gifts in the church, and we should bestow more honor upon those that are seemingly less honorable (I Corinthians 12:22-23).

III John 3 tells us that God wishes above all things that His children prosper and be in health even as our souls prosper. Doesn't it make sense that if God made this wish that He also made provisions for His own wish to come true? More so, this is the assurance that within every person, there is a gift that God placed on the inside of each of us to develop and package properly for our great wealth and success while we are on earth. Deuteronomy 28 tells us that we are to have plenty to establish our covenant with God and that we should lend and not borrow. What a great reflection of the glory of God the world will see when the members of the body of Christ will show the world a blessed people, not an oppressed people.

The condition of the church when Bishop Hash became chief overseer was one of devout belief, but little fruit bearing. Some of the best gospel singers and musicians that anyone could ever find came from the church, but they lacked knowledge of how to professionally package themselves and understand the business of music. They felt that they were successfully singing when they could arouse the congregation to shout uncontrollably. As a Black race, music has always been important to us, but when it only tends to feed our emotions and we do not worship our creator, then it's just tinkling sounds.

My sister, Delilah, started a praise team and taught them scriptural songs. Everyone thought we were trying to get too much like the White Pentecostal churches, because the beat of many of the scriptural songs was different from the fast songs that we typically sang in our church. The uncontrollable shouting or as some would call it, dancing in the spirit, seemingly turned into a bunny hop. And when she began to teach worship songs and sung them in a spiritual language to enter into the throne room of God's heart, they really thought she had flipped.

It's sad, but true, that we were people who had been full gospel Christians for more than half a century, but had never been taught how to really worship our God. We thought that we had to feel *a quickening of the spirit* that caused us to foam at the mouth and shake uncontrollably in order to have the Holy Spirit, also known as the Holy Ghost. When we started teaching the congregation that the Holy Spirit is a gift given to every believer and that we have a spiritual prayer language to communicate with God in the spirit, we were accused of teaching people how to speak in tongues.

When I was a young girl growing up in the church, we used to have Tuesday night tarry services whereby we would go to the altar and call out repeatedly "Jesus, Jesus, Jesus" for hours trying to get the Holy Ghost. The older women who were called the mothers of the church would tell you ,"Press child, press! Let it all go! Give it all up!"

Some people did this for many years trying to feel the quickening that they saw the others demonstrating and acquire the fancy shouting or dancing in the spirit steps. They gave up make-up, jewelry, pants, going to movies, ball games, friends, their homes, money, and everything because they thought that that was what it took to be holy and to receive the Holy Ghost.

Looking back at it now, it seems ridiculous, but guess what? There are still many pastors who are holding on to that belief and have a faithful few following them. Are you one of them? It's amazing how hard it is to give up something that has been attached to you for so long, although it does not bear fruit.

Motivate the People to Catch the Vision

Helping people grow and taking them where God wants you to take them requires that they have an understanding of what the vision is all about. God commanded Moses to explain to the elders of Israel why he had come so they would cooperate with him in accomplishing God's vision. Without that understanding, there would be no transformation; the people would still operate in the "slavery-mentality" from which God wanted them liberated. Without that mental emancipation, they could not enjoy the liberty God was bringing to them.

This I saw my father do as he tried to bring change in our church and in churches in the Triad area. Through teaching, Bishop Hash not only taught the people what God had showed him but motivated them to buy into that vision. He instructed them and the vision of the church was made available to all members in various forms. Every member was given a copy of the vision for the church. It was printed in the visitors' brochure and in all church ministry manuals. It was laminated on cards and distributed to every adult, youth, and child. The vision was also designed into a full-color picture and displayed where everyone could see it each time they came to church.

Every Sunday, Bishop said something about the vision. An audiotape containing the vision was given to every person who came to the church the first time. He encouraged the song ministers in the church to write songs based on the vision. There was such a saturation of the vision that everyone understood exactly where the church was heading. That is very important in order for people to understand exactly what is expected of them. They will also know what God wants to do for them and with them. Even though all of this seems like a huge task, every church leader must strive to promote the vision to get the people right and ready to embark on the journey to freedom.

The sixth chapter of Hebrews explains how to tell the vision.

> Therefore leaving the principles of the doctrine of Christ, let us go on unto perfection; not laying again the foundation of repentance from dead works, and of faith toward God, Of the doctrine of baptisms, and of laying on of hands, and of resurrection of the dead, and of eternal judgment. And this will

we do, if God permit. For it is impossible for those who were once enlightened, and have tasted of the heavenly gift, and were made partakers of the Holy Ghost, And have tasted the good Word of God, and the powers of the world to come,

If they shall fall away, to renew them again unto repentance; seeing they crucify to themselves the Son of God afresh, and put him to an open shame. For the earth which drinketh in the rain that cometh oft upon it, and bringeth forth herbs meet for them by whom it is dressed, receiveth blessing from God: But that which beareth thorns and briers is rejected, and is nigh unto cursing; whose end is to be burned. But, beloved, we are persuaded better things of you, and things that accompany salvation, though we thus speak. For God is not unrighteous to forget your work and labour of love, which ye have shewed toward his name, in that ye have ministered to the saints, and do minister. And we desire that every one of you do shew the same diligence to the full assurance of hope unto the end: That ye be not slothful, but followers of them who through faith and patience inherit the promises.

For when God made promise to Abraham, because he could swear by no greater, he sware by himself, Saying, Surely blessing I will bless thee, and multiplying I will multiply thee. And so, after he had patiently endured, he obtained the promise. For men verily swear by the greater: and an oath for confirmation is to them an end of all strife. Wherein God, willing more abundantly to shew unto the heirs of promise the immutability of his counsel, confirmed it by an oath: That by two immutable things, in which it was impossible for God to lie, we might have a strong consolation, who have fled for refuge to lay hold upon the hope set before us:

Which hope we have as an anchor of the soul, both sure and stedfast, and which entereth into that within the veil; Whither the forerunner is for us entered, even Jesus, made an high priest for ever after the order of Melchisedec.

Hebrews 6:1-20

Develop the People's Talents

One important aspect of developing people is developing their talents. God gives talents for service. God adds to the Church daily. Why? The answer is simple - to staff His vision. Within every congregation is a multiplicity of talents. The wise church leader is the one who sets up his infrastructure to help his members first discover their God-given talents and provide opportunities for their development as well. Ephesians 4 tells us that people desire fulfillment and when they are placed in the body of Christ where they fit, they excel. They excel not because someone is needed to do the job and so they do it, but because the job is their purpose, their divine gift, and ministry call. Their gift is where they fit in the body. From cutting the grass on the church campus to cleaning the restrooms, the gifts within the people spread throughout and fill every need for total operations of the vision of God.

In every city that you go to, the phone company sends you a big, thick book called the yellow pages and it is filled with gifted people who have packaged their gifts, their professions, and are presenting them to the world to receive great riches. I'd dare to say that over 75% of those business owners do not know to give God honor for their gifts and talents.

Signs should follow the believers and therefore every believer should reach within himself or herself to determine the dominant gifts and talents that are to be packaged and presented to the world. We, in the body of Christ, must position ourselves for the promises of God. In I Kings 17, Elijah had to go to a *specific* house and to a *specific* brook to acquire his blessing.

> And the word of the LORD came unto him, saying, Get thee hence, and turn thee eastward, and hide thyself by the brook Cherith, that is before Jordan. And it shall be, that thou shalt drink of the brook; and I have commanded the ravens to feed thee there. So he went and did according unto the word of the LORD: for he went and dwelt by the brook Cherith,

that is before Jordan.

And the ravens brought him bread and flesh in the morning, and bread and flesh in the evening; and he drank of the brook. And it came to pass after a while, that the brook dried up, because there had been no rain in the land. And the word of the LORD came unto him, saying,

Arise, get thee to Zarephath, which belongeth to Zidon, and dwell there: behold, I have commanded a widow woman there to sustain thee. So he arose and went to Zarephath. And when he came to the gate of the city, behold, the widow woman was there gathering of sticks: and he called to her, and said, Fetch me, I pray thee, a little water in a vessel, that I may drink. And as she was going to fetch it, he called to her, and said, Bring me, I pray thee, a morsel of bread in thine hand. And she said, As the LORD thy God liveth, I have not a cake, but an handful of meal in a barrel, and a little oil in a cruse: and, behold, I am gathering two sticks, that I may go in and dress it for me and my son, that we may eat it, and die.

And Elijah said unto her, Fear not; go and do as thou hast said: but make me thereof a little cake first, and bring it unto me, and after make for thee and for thy son. For thus saith the LORD God of Israel, The barrel of meal shall not waste, neither shall the cruse of oil fail, until the day that the LORD sendeth rain upon the earth. And she went and did according to the saying of Elijah: and she, and he, and her house, did eat many days. And the barrel of meal wasted not, neither did the cruse of oil fail, according to the word of the LORD, which he spake by Elijah.

I Kings 17:2-16

Develop the People's Character

The most outstanding way people show they belong to Christ is by exhibiting Christ-like character. Even though many of us may not walk in the powerful healing ministries of Oral Roberts, Kathryn Khulman, or Benny Hinn, or the powerful evangelistic ministries of Billy Graham, or the missionary accomplishments of T. L Osborn, or the great work that Bishop Hash did in the Triad area, each of us must exhibit the character of Jesus Christ to be identified as children of the heavenly Father.

As a church leader, never forget to ask yourself:

- What is the lifestyle of my worship leader?
- What is the character of my prayer leader?
- What is the integrity of my youth leader?

In an era in which talent is elevated over character, church leaders have serious issues about which to answer to God one day.

If guidelines aren't necessary, then why do fortune 500 corporations have operations manuals and human resource departments? Why do we frown upon guidelines in the church and yet without them, we would not have any order in our day-to-day lives; therefore, even more so, we should apply the guidelines from the Word of God as our instructions for the character that we should project to the world. Integrity is doing the right thing when no one is looking.

The world must see the character of God in our mannerisms, our conversations, and in everything that we do. In Exodus 18, Jethro gave Moses specific guidelines on how to choose able men to help him carry out the vision that God gave him. They were to bare the burden with him and assist him, but not to take over.

[19] Hearken now unto my voice, I will give thee counsel, and God shall be with thee: Be thou for the people to God-ward, that thou mayest bring the causes unto God: [20] And thou shalt teach them ordinances and laws, and shalt shew them the way wherein they must walk, and the work that they must do. [21] Moreover thou shalt provide out of all the people able

men, such as fear God, men of truth, hating covetousness; and place such over them, to be rulers of thousands, and rulers of hundreds, rulers of fifties, and rulers of tens: [22] *And let them judge the people at all seasons: and it shall be, that every great matter they shall bring unto thee, but every small matter they shall judge: so shall it be easier for thyself, and they shall bear the burden with thee.*
Exodus 18:19-22

Our country is run according to a specific organizational structure. From the President to every layer of our political and judicial system, there is a specific person and a specialized team to get the job done. Structure in the Church must be absolutely solid according to the standards that God outlined in His manual, the Bible.

Counsel the People by God's Word

No effective church growth can take place without an effective counseling ministry. Counseling does what cannot be done from the pulpit. A good counseling program meets people at their exact point of need and takes them through a process: teaching them how to apply practical principles in accordance with God's word, identifying their particular problems, and walking them through the solutions by the Word of God. Senior pastors who are still counseling all of their members are stifling their own growth, and will eventually experience total burnout and an unbalanced life, just as Moses did.

Therefore, pastors must delegate the oversight of pastoral counseling to a qualified associate pastor or leader. As a matter of fact, it protects senior pastors from liability by removing them from this role if they are not qualified.

Wonderful organizations such as Associates in Christian Counseling are available for churches to direct their members for professional biblical as well as clinical counseling. The natural and the supernatural combined bring total healing.

When Jethro saw how Moses was burning himself out by listening to the problems of the people from sun up to sun down, he told Moses in Exodus 18:14, "This is a bad thing that you do *to the people.*" Notice he did not say *for the people*, because it was not fair to the people for him to heap all of that responsibility upon himself when he had able men and women ready to help him carry the burden. He could not go to the mountain and hear from God in peace because there was no order set in the camp. Many pastors are not involved within their community organizations or cannot ever get away from their ministries because they are afraid that while they are away, someone will take their place.

This is ludicrous! When God gave Moses the Ten Commandments, He was simply trying to help Moses establish order and direction for the people to abide by. He was setting up governments. There will always be people who debate the pastor's leadership because people are on different spiritual maturity levels. But when a pastor who knows without a doubt that his vision is directly from God, and not due to ego or rebellion, and when he has taken the time to bring his inner circle together to establish the government of the church, then he will experience two things: he will free himself to see the vision manifest and he will be empowered to gain a balance in his personal life with his spouse and children.

What would it profit a pastor to have a large ministry and yet lose his health, his family, and especially his children?

Develop the People into Leaders

The people in the Church are the great company that God has given to publish His Word. To go far in your ministry, start early to develop leadership in your people. This involves not only leadership seminars but also to provide opportunities for leadership in the church as well as in the community. Jesus taught the disciples and then He sent them out to practice what He had taught them. Send your people out to evangelize, pray for the sick, and cast out demons. In doing service, they develop the leadership potential which is already within them when they come to you. Do not be afraid to train and delegate. A great leader understands the value of duplicating himself by teaching, training, and coaching able leaders; therefore, the vision becomes broader within the four walls of the church as well as within the community, city, state, and the world.

When Paul sent Timothy to represent him in the city of Corinth, it was the same as if he himself were there because Timothy knew exactly what to say to the church in Corinth. When the leaders have been trained how to articulate the vision that God has set for the church, then they will all say the same things that the senior pastor says when they represent the church in city and community organizations.

Leadership classes can be added to the Sunday morning school of ministry or Christian education hour to make it convenient for the leaders to be successful with completing them. Each department should have a head leader and an assistant; therefore, they can rotate attending the class and yet there will always be a leader on duty for every position. Be cautious about over-extending the number of days required for leaders to be away from their family and jobs. You must create a win-win situation if you want the leaders to be loyal to the vision of the church.

The word "leadership" is often misunderstood and is used to gain clout and status. The Word of God says that there should not be any schisms among us. In God's eye, the leader of cutting the church grass and keeping the water fountains clean is equally as important as any other leader in the church. The promises in the Bible are for every believer.

God rewards diligence. The parking attendants diligently parking the cars as unto the Lord will receive as great a reward as any other ministry gift such as a pastor, prophet, evangelist, and apostle.

There are no big "I's" and little "u's." I Corinthians 12 tells us that all gifts are placed in the church by the same Lord and the same Spirit, and we should bestow more honor upon those gifts that are seemingly less honorable .

> Now there are diversities of gifts, but *the same Spirit.* And there are differences of administrations, but *the same Lord.*

And there are diversities of operations, but it is *the same God* which worketh all in all. But the manifestation of the Spirit is given to every man to profit withal. For to one is given by the Spirit the word of wisdom; to another the word of knowledge by *the same Spirit*; To another faith by *the same Spirit*; to another the gifts of healing by *the same Spirit*; To another the working of miracles; to another prophecy; to another discerning of spirits; to another divers kinds of tongues; to another the interpretation of tongues:

But all these worketh that *one and the selfsame Spirit*, dividing to every man severally as he will. For as the body is one, and hath many members, and all the members of that one body, being many, are one body: so also is Christ. For by *one Spirit* are we all baptized into one body, whether we be Jews or Gentiles, whether we be bond or free; and have been all made to drink into *one Spirit*. For the body is not one member, but many.

If the foot shall say, Because I am not the hand, I am not of the body; is it therefore not of the body? And if the ear shall say, Because I am not the eye, I am not of the body; is it therefore not of the body? If the whole body were an eye, where were the hearing? If the whole were hearing, where were the smelling?

But now hath God set the members every one of them in the body, as it hath pleased him. And if they were all one member, where were the body? But now are they many members, yet but *one body*. And the eye cannot say unto the hand, I have no need of thee: nor again the head to the feet, I have no need of you. *Nay, much more those members of the body, which seem to be more feeble, are necessary: And those members of the body, which we think to be less honourable, upon these we bestow more abundant honour; and our uncomely parts have more abundant comeliness.* For our comely parts have no need: but God hath tempered the body together, having given more abundant honour to that part which lacked. That there should be no schism in the body; but that the members should have the same care one for another. And whether one member suffer, all the members suffer with it; or one member be honoured, all the members rejoice with it.

I Corinthians 12:4-26

When attention is placed on the development of the people, then and only then does the church become stronger: individuals and their family relationships become stronger and they learn how to turn their talents into businesses.

The consistency of people giving all on different levels adds up supernaturally to meet the budget and the workload of the church operations. Eventually change is inevitable:

- The lifestyles of the members change
- The offerings increase across the board
- The members are healed
- The cars in the parking lot change to Mercedes, BMW's, etc,
- The members testify of taking luxury vacations
- The youth testify of going to colleges and universities
- Families become strong

The people in the pews become leaders not only in the church, but also in their homes, at their jobs, in their neighborhoods, and every place in every aspect of their lives.

Your church members must show the world the good, the acceptable, and the perfect will of God. The best example to the world is to be living epistles of the Word of God.

A Balanced Lifestyle

I contemplated whether I should reveal this very private aspect of my life, but I realized that unless I am totally transparent to my readers, then I would only be giving advice about *what I have read and heard* from others, rather than *what I have actually lived.* I have mentioned many times throughout this book that there are as many divorces and broken homes in the Church as there are in the non-churched world. *Even though all of the ministry goals I accomplished during my twenty-four years as a Church Administrator have been great, looking back at my life I discovered that during all of that time, my life was totally unbalanced.* Even though I do not regret anything that I ever did or gave to help people, *my only regret is that I failed to have more balance in my family relationships and to pursue my own dreams as I was helping others.*

A good friend of mine once told me that I was so busy doing the work of the Lord that I did not know the Lord of the work. Of course I was offended. However, when I became totally honest with myself, I realized that I had worked so hard each day that I was too tired to pray, study the Bible, or even enjoy quality time with my family at the end of the day. As a result, I found myself successful in the Lord's house, yet failed in my own.

On March 14, 2003, I got the courage to leave my job and start a consultant firm. One year later, my grown children convinced me that we should draw closer together as a family and make up for some of the time that we had lost as they were growing up. *I soon realized that I was being given a second chance to start my life over. I'm healthy, tall, and beautiful, so here I am!* I found the inner courage to launch out to start over again, because I realized that if I didn't do it now while I am still young enough, I may not ever get another chance.

My son, Sean, is a very successful businessman in real estate. My daughter, Tameeka, is a professional singer and model. I am a writer, church and business consultant to pastors and church leaders, and the owner of a thriving home-based marketing business. My children and I are now working together as a team to establish generational wealth for our children's children as God has commanded all Christians to do. My daddy taught me that making money is like a three- legged stool: you should have it coming in at least three ways, so if one leg falls off, you always have two more on which to stand.

Each day, I now ask myself, "What is the best use of my time?" If an activity or relationship is not moving my family and me towards accomplishing our family vision, then I recognize it as an outside interruption, which according to Ecclesiastes 3:1-22 is designed to steal the God-given gift of time from me and therefore I absolutely refuse to invest any time in it. During my daily devotion, I have a board meeting with my angels and give them assignments to go throughout the earth to bring the people, finances, and other means needed to keep our family vision moving in the direction of greatness that God has predestined for our family.

I believe this spells balance!

Protect your leaders from becoming super humans and taking on more than they can handle. Don't allow them to experience burnout or lose their spouses or children while they are trying to do the "Lord's" work. There are just as many or more divorces among pastors and church leaders as there are anywhere else. What kind of statement does this make to our children and to the world when they see families splitting who profess to be children of God?

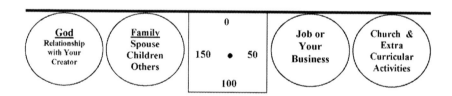

God is the source of our life. God should be involved with everything we begin. He knows every second of every moment of our lives; therefore, common sense tells us to always involve Him in even the simplest things that we do. Throughout the Bible, we see structure and order. Look at the master plan that God used to create the earth and everything in it. "In the beginning" is the same thing as beginning everything with God, and then He will direct your path.

In the beginning God created the heaven and the earth. And

the earth was without form, and void; and darkness was upon the face of the deep. And the Spirit of God moved upon the face of the waters. And God said, Let there be light: and there was light. And God saw the light, that it was good: and God divided the light from the darkness. And God called the light Day, and the darkness he called Night. And the evening and the morning were the first day
Genesis 1:1-5

Read the rest of Genesis 1 as well as Genesis 2 to see how important order is in our lives.

I'm amazed that, even now in the twenty-first century with the thousands of time management tools available, I encounter church leaders and pastors who still don't have a structured method of planning their day-to-day activities. I'm even more amazed at how much frustration I see going on between pastors and church leaders and they don't even have a master plan to get from point A to Z.

Many pastors fail to write down the vision that is in their heart. They're busy as they can be and all the while a few faithful leaders are experiencing burnout and family break-ups, and all because of *lack of knowledge*!

- Call in the Church Administrators!
- Call in the consultants!
- Invest in your vision!
- Invest in your leaders!
- Invest in yourself!

Continue to go to conferences, but what will you do when you return home to your church? Administrators and consultants will work directly with you one-on-one to help you make professional assessments and strategies to get you from point A-to-Z of your vision.

If your body is sick, you go to the doctor. Even more so, if you are experiencing difficulty in your church or business, you must be willing to pay the price for the intellectual property of the experts.

CHAPTER THREE

Strategy Three

Organize for the Vision
"Let all things be done in order"

Identify Leadership for the Vision

God's plans and purposes are bigger than any man and He never expects any man to carry the burden of His vision alone. Whether we are talking about the universal Church or a local church, God's principles do not change. He has prepared for Himself a team to accomplish His vision. That underscores the inevitability of developing people for the vision. If any leader refuses to consciously develop people, then the people will not be ready when needed for leadership.

> The Lord gave the word: great was the company of those that published it.
>
> Psalm 68:11

> And he gave some, apostles; and some, prophets; and some, evangelists; and some, pastors and teachers; For the

perfecting of the saints, for the work of the ministry, for the edifying of the body of Christ...

Ephesians 4:11-12

We live in an era when we falsely interpret messages about carrying out a ministry. Many see big ministries and all they see is the founder of the ministry. Perhaps there is such an overemphasis on the role of the leader that we overlook the fact that God called many people to stand with the leader. God's principle for carrying out His vision has not changed one bit. Read the following examples from the Old and the New Testaments.

Old Testament Foundations

Today, in ministry and corporate organizations alike, we hear clichés like *division of labor*, *team management*, and several others. This charge to involve others in leadership has its roots in the Old Testament. The advice Jethro gave Moses introduced this principle in leadership and it is as vibrant and relevant today as it was then.

> And it came to pass on the morrow, that Moses sat to judge the people: and the people stood by Moses from the morning unto the evening. *And when Moses' father in law saw all that he did to the people, he said, What is this thing that thou doest to the people (not for, but to)? why sittest thou thyself alone, and all the people stand by thee from morning unto even?* And Moses said unto his father in law, Because the people come unto me to enquire of God: When they have a matter, they come unto me; and I judge between one and another, and I do make them know the statutes of God, and his laws.
>
> *And Moses' father in law said unto him, The thing that thou doest is not good. Thou wilt surely wear away, both thou, and this people that is with thee: for this thing is too heavy for thee; thou art not able to perform it thyself alone. Hearken now unto my voice, I will give thee counsel, and God shall be with thee: Be thou for the people to God-ward,*

that thou mayest bring the causes unto God: And thou shalt teach them ordinances and laws, and shalt shew them the way wherein they must walk, and the work that they must do.

Moreover thou shalt provide out of all the people able men, (guidelines) such as fear God, men of truth, hating covetousness; and place such over them, to be rulers of thousands, and rulers of hundreds, rulers of fifties, and rulers of tens: And let them judge the people at all seasons: and it shall be, that every great matter they shall bring unto thee, but every small matter they shall judge: so shall it be easier for thyself, and they shall bear the burden with thee.
Exodus 18:13-22

New Testament Continuation of the Principle

The principle of involving others in various levels of leadership is continued in the New Testament.

And in those days, when the number of the disciples was multiplied, there arose a murmuring of the Grecians against the Hebrews, because their widows were neglected in the daily ministration. *Then the twelve called the multitude of the disciples unto them, and said, It is not reason that we should leave the Word of God, and serve tables. Wherefore, brethren, look ye out among you seven men of honest report, full of the Holy Ghost and wisdom, whom we may appoint over this business. But we will give ourselves continually to prayer, and to the ministry of the word.* And the saying pleased the whole multitude: and they chose Stephen, a man full of faith and of the Holy Ghost, and Philip, and Prochorus, and Nicanor, and Timon, and Parmenas, and Nicolas a proselyte of Antioch: Whom they set before the apostles: and when they had prayed, they laid their hands on them. And the Word of God increased; and the number of the disciples multiplied in Jerusalem greatly; and a great company of the priests were obedient to the faith.
Acts 6:1-7

Paul affirms the principle when he wrote the following message to the church in Ephesus:

> He that descended is the same also that ascended up far above all heavens, that he might fill all things.) And he gave some, apostles; and some, prophets; and some, evangelists; and some, pastors and teachers; For the perfecting of the saints, for the work of the ministry, for the edifying of the body of Christ: Till we all come in the unity of the faith, (become leaders) and of the knowledge of the Son of God, unto a perfect man, unto the measure of the stature of the fulness of Christ...
>
> Ephesians 4:10-13

This is what is commonly referred to as the "five-fold ministry." It identifies that a healthy church needs these major ministries. Most churches today however do not have them. Most have a leader who is exalted above everyone, and in most cases he or she is the only one that seems to matter in the entire ministry.

If a pastor's wife is shy, timid, and withdrawn, she is showing signs of neglect abuse by her husband and rejection by the church members. Worse yet she could be overbearing and scornful because of the hurt, anger, and negative attention she has received. These women are left feeling lonely, unimportant, and insecure. In either case, these outward exhibits of ungodly character reflect inner turmoil, confusion, conflict, and sometimes rage. Is it any surprise what kind of Christians we are turning out today?

God's provision for His vision goes beyond what is called the five-fold ministry. There is a whole array of other gifts and talents that God has provided to support the vision.

> Now ye are the body of Christ, and members in particular. And God hath set some in the church, first apostles, secondarily prophets, thirdly teachers, after that miracles, then gifts of healings, helps, governments, diversities of tongues. Are all apostles? are all prophets? are all teachers? are all workers of miracles? Have all the gifts of healing? do all

speak with tongues? do all interpret? But covet earnestly the best gifts: and yet shew I unto you a more excellent way.

1 Corinthians 12:27-31

The excellent way, described in I Corinthians 13, is to love and develop God's people. You must realize that no matter how intelligent they may look, the people sitting in your pews bring their personalities and backgrounds with them. They may be well dressed up on the outside and wear fur coats and diamond rings, but they are still carrying emotional hurts from life experiences.

People will continue to search for fulfillment until you teach them how to apply the Word of God to obtain complete healing in all areas of their lives.

Develop Your Church Ministries

Children's and Youth Ministry

Everyone is familiar with the alarming statistics of children killing their playmates, friends, siblings, and even their parents. Not only are teenagers addicted to drugs, alcohol, and sex, but small children are too. Statistics show there are higher percentages of families with absent fathers who leave their wives to be single mothers, carrying the entire load.

Knowing this means that a pastor should be concerned about his flock seven days a week, not just on Sunday. The children's church should be a refuge for kids and teenagers for after school programs, tutorial classes, young entrepreneurial classes, dance classes, sports programs, and any other benefit that the world offers. This keeps our children in a safe, Christian environment.

A dear friend of our family, who the children of St. Peter's have known as Auntie Pat, put her whole heart into developing the children's ministry at St. Peter's. She passionately tells how she knows her purpose and does not want to do anything else in the body of Christ but to develop children. Her gift made room for her and now she is a professional certified storyteller and travels across the country thrilling children with stories that build godly value and character in them.

Men's and Women's Ministry

Pastors must understand who the people really are in their pews. Statistical reports reveal that the thousands of men and women who are incarcerated or are addicted to drugs have young children who are subjected to physical, sexual, mental, and emotional abuse and neglect each day. Because of the vicious cycle of poverty and various addictions, these children are forced to raise themselves and many grow up psychologically handicapped and emotionally crippled. I was fortunate to have acquired a B.S. degree in Special Education, which helped me to understand how a person's personality is formed. Our bodies and minds are so miraculously created. Stored up in our emotions are personality traits that stem from third, fourth, and fifth generations. Physical illnesses as well as emotional illnesses are hereditary.

I know that you've heard people say that they are shy just like their mother was.

Well, if something such as shyness keeps one from moving forward in the things God established for His children, then shyness certainly did not come from God. It's a spirit that does not belong to the men and women of God. *The Bible says that the righteous is bold as a lion.* Shyness stems from fear and low self-esteem. It is not cute to see a grown adult being shy, having a low self-esteem, short-fused, or any unacceptable behavior. As long as your members carry these hereditary traits, they will never walk in completeness.

Men and women's ministries should be more than cute socials. They should be developmental opportunities that teach men and women practical biblical life skills and how to apply the Word of God, their testimonies, and the blood of Jesus to live a life of success. You see, God took away all of the excuses for us to carry these things such as bitterness and pain from childhood hurts, rejection from a broken marriage, or any other curse; He paid the supreme sacrifice and sent His son, Jesus, on the cross to defeat all the principalities of the world.

Luke 6:38 tells us that the way to keep something is to give it away. There's a song that I used to sing to my children that goes like this:

> Love is something if you give it away, give it away, give it away.
> Love is something if you give it away; you end up having more.
> It's just like a magic penny; hold it tight and you won't have many,
> But if you lend it, give it, you'll have so many, they'll roll all over the floor.
> So love is something if you give it away, give it away, give it away.
> Love is something if you give it away, you'll end up having more!

Men and Women's departments should collaborate with other community help programs such as the American Cancer Society, teenage pregnancy programs, and the like. This not only gives the women and men of the church meaningful ministry opportunities, but it also bridges the gap between the church and the community.

These connections become evangelistic opportunities for your congregation. The success of how your members overcame their emotional hurts is a conversation (testimony) to those community organizations with whom they come in contact. When the women of the church are involved in walk-a-thons for breast cancer, they have the opportunity through their conversations (testimonies) of how God healed them. This is true evangelism.

You see, it's not always necessary to preach and quote scriptures to show the world what God has done. Your life is a testimony and it should be a reflection of the glory of God.

My mother had breast cancer when she was seventy-eight years old. Although she had surgery to remove the lump, she is completely cured and now has a testimony to share. Everybody knows Mother Hash. There's not hardly a clerk in any store or restaurant in Winston Salem that does not know her and respect her. If she sees a clerk or waitress with a frown, she makes a point to make them smile before she leaves. She will tell them how blessed they are to be in the land of the living and she always leaves them laughing. She has favor everywhere she goes. She is a reflection of the glory of God.

Family Enrichment Ministry

Make your children, youth, men, and women's programs evolve into a total family enrichment center for infants to adults. Previously, I mentioned that many of the things that God puts in the heart of a pastor are, in reality, community services. With some concrete business strategies, your children and youth's programs can become part of a community center that can qualify for grants to fund the entire project. There are consultants available to do feasibility studies and master plans to make sure your demographic area is marketable for such programs. In other words, if a church or organization within a ten-block radius from your church were already offering these programs, it would be wiser to collaborate with them. Use your revenue to start other programs that are not being offered in your community.

Bridge the Gap Between Your Church and Your Community

This is another reason why it is important for pastors and church leaders to serve on community boards and to attend the city mayor's prayer sessions. By sitting at the table with the decision makers of your city, you get first hand information of future city development projects and you become knowledgeable of potential funding for programs that may fit your church's demographic area.

Step Out of the Church Box for a Second. I believe this is a good place to mention this in this book, so here goes. Take a look at the global picture of what is happening to bridge the gap between the Church and the twenty-first century public. Statistics show that billions of dollars are made in the music and entertainment industry and fourteen to thirty year olds are the major consumers. What does this say to us? Entertainers in the Hip Hop and Rock music industry, among others, have found a way to strategically put gospel lines within their songs that are being played in every youth center and club throughout the country. So now the message of the gospel is being heard not only in the Church, but also across all lines.

These people are able to reach those who may never step into a church, but they cannot leave earth saying that they never heard the gospel. Yes, statistics are high for teenage pregnancies and incarceration, so wouldn't it be wise to use the same vehicle that put them there to pull them out? It's almost subliminal, but it is happening. Troubled people didn't get that way overnight, so we will not see a great change overnight; however, with continual use of innovative strategies, change is inevitable.

Instead of condemning the Hip-Hop and Rock entertainers, who have so much influence over this generation, why not team up with them to help attack the situation? Pastors, we must get our heads out of the sand. Many people condemned some of the gospel singers for their style of music and said that they were selling out, but that is a very narrow-minded statement. When a person stays in a small closed-in box, their opinions are based only on what they have seen and experienced within their box.

And if I might, and I will might because this is my book, I will also give my viewpoint of the statements that a well-known actor said about Blacks taking some responsibility for the high statistics of Black fathers and youth in prison. There are numerous governmental programs that are supposedly in place to help change this, and yet the statistics keep climbing. These incarcerated fathers and youth are ours, so we must change things within our homes and other places that touch their lives to snatch them back into the types of morals and values that our parents taught us.

I have to admit that since March 14, 2003, when I got the courage to step out of my box as Administrator of St. Peter's World Outreach Center, my paradigms have broadened and my viewpoint opened up to understand what is really taking place in this big world. When I said, "Father, send me to the nations," I really did not know at that time what those words really meant. Since that time, I have had the privilege of being exposed to people from many different countries, which has broadened my paradigms and helped me form opinions based on an understanding of other cultural values and not just my own. So, again, I say to you, step out of the box and observe what is really taking place in the world, and then you can form a more broader and accurate opinion.

Your congregation depends on you to lead them. Pastors have the power to lead hundreds, even thousands of people into a specific direction. You owe it to your congregation to study and hear from God which direction He has for the Church. And as you step outside of your box, avoid giving them a flat "yes" or "no" to anything, including politics, which is another subject altogether.

Develop a Vibrant Helps Ministry

As a means to gradually implement change in the local church, start a Ministry of Helps (MOH) department. Rev. Buddy Bell was instrumental in assisting us to write our first Ministry of Helps manual, which included the church guidelines and protocol. Ministry of Helps serves as the spiritual gifts and is founded on I Corinthians 12, Romans 12, and Ephesians 4. The Human Resource office sets up the following procedures:

a. Recruitment and Placement - Make sure that the members are placed in the body *where they fit according to their spiritual gifts* so that they will experience meaningful ministry.

b. Training - Conduct classes to teach every member about their gifts and how their gifts are their divine connection with their Creator to bring about the promises that He has given them on earth. The MOH office also makes sure that each department has a training manual with which to train new members as they are placed in their respective departments.

c. Screening - Make sure that the ministry is legally protected in placing people in ministry areas such as finances, children's ministries, transportation, food services, etc. by conducting a criminal and/or health background check. Develop the guidelines, policies, and procedures for participation such as dress codes, etc.

d. Awards and Recognition - Make sure that all volunteers are given fair recognition. Assist the Education Director in conducting the mass graduation ceremony for the School of Ministry graduates.
e. Evaluations - Establish the annual evaluation module for all volunteers.
f. Documentation - Make sure that all documentation is properly maintained and filed.

Gifts in the Church

God requires us to do His work on earth; therefore, He places gifts in the church. We are the church. I Corinthians 12:1-27 tells us that all gifts come from God. I Corinthians 12:28 describes that the ministry of helps and administration are equally as important to the ministry as the other gifts, or they would not have all been written in the same sentence. The gift of diligently cleaning the church merits the same reward as the prophets and teachers, for God is a rewarder to them that diligently seek Him.

According to Ephesians 4:11-16, God placed gifts in the church for specific purposes:

- for the equipping (teaching) of the saints for the work of the ministry
- for the edifying of the body of Christ
- till we *all* come to the unity of the faith
- that we should no longer be children tossed to and fro
- that we can *all* speak the truth in love
- that we may grow up in *all* things into Him Who is the head – Christ
- from whom the *whole body* jointly knitted together by what *every* joint supplies

According to Luke 6:46-49, Leaders must know they know that they have heard from God in making decisions about His work or the decisions will not bear long lasting eternal fruit. Matthew 16:13-19 tell us that flesh and blood cannot reveal spiritual things to you, only our Father in heaven can. Every facet of your ministry must be built on the Word of God and prayer.

The Age of Technology

Over the years, several software programs have evolved that help to maintain a vibrant helps office. If your ministry is a non-profit 501c3 organization, then the volunteer hours that your members give is valued at approximately $20 per hour. By keeping documentation, these hours can be used as matching funds if you needed to apply for a grant. Sometimes lending institutions even request this data. Software for the Ministry of Helps and Human Resource offices also enables the ministry to be able to connect to phone calling systems, whereby the leaders can have the proper demographics of single or married parents with children, racial diversity, gender, age, professions, location, and more.

Say, for example, you need to do a project that involves all of the carpenters of the church, or for any other project, then your software program would be able to make a personal phone call or letter to all the carpenters. This is the same thing that Aaron did for Moses when he organized the children of Israel to leave Egypt. He grouped all of the people according to their trades and dialects.

As a result of biblical teachings and structure, there is practically nothing that the church is in need of, because God places the people in the church for the purpose of completing His vision. In return, the peoples' personal visions for their families will be fulfilled. This could not have happened if Bishop Hash would have been a selfish man and used the ministry for his personal gain. He used the same principle that he taught his people for his own personal success as an example to others that God was truly his source.

Human Resource Office for Staff and Volunteers

The Ministry of Helps and Human Resource offices are instrumental in developing a generic development training manual for all staff, leaders and volunteer workers. This maintains the cohesiveness of the overall operations of the ministry. Remember, your aim is to create one image, your core; therefore, you cannot allow everyone to do it his or her way.

The Ministry of Helps and the Human Resource offices should establish the check and balance system for overall training. There should be a systematic training process for every new member who comes into the church. Everyone should understand and be able to speak the vision of the church to project the core of the ministry. Again, this is a corporate process. When I visited the Holy Land, I had lunch at a McDonalds. They followed the same process as any other McDonalds in the world. Why? Because the franchise manuals tell them that if they do things in exactly the way their manual outlines, they are guaranteed success. God's Word is our guarantee!

Training and Operations Manuals
The Ministry of Helps and Human Resource offices also must write training manuals on topics such as conflict resolution, time management, project management, how to facilitate a meeting, the art of delegation, interpersonal relationship skills, etc. The bi-monthly and quarterly leadership meetings should include staff development training in order to keep all of the staff and leaders in one accord and to empower them to conduct themselves according to the integrity and standards of the overall church. One image, one people, one voice, one message, all striving together for the faith of the Gospel. This management strategy also enables you to create a model that can be duplicated from city to city and state to state.

Pastors must absolutely know what is best for the vision of the house that God placed them over. At the end of the day, it boils down to teaching people who they are in Christ, that they are filled with gifts, and that they are destined for success when they tap into the reservoir of God.

Outside sources such as student teachers from the local colleges can provide additional skilled free help for your day care centers, before and after school programs, clerical assistants, and most any field of study. Many organizations such as the Urban League and the Retired Seniors Volunteer Program (RSVP) also contribute free workforce for your programs.

Enhance Your Administrative Support
In following the injunction to do all things decently and in

order, Bishop Hash made some changes to enhance the overall administrative support for the ministry. He hired an accountant, a full time church secretary, a financial clerk, and an administrator. This changed the old format where the deacons would stand before the church to open praise and worship, receive the offering, and then also handle the business aspects of the church. No disrespect to them, but many of them could not manage their own budgets. They were great Christian men, but they simply were not businessmen and did not have the administrative skills required by a progressive, growing church.

Today's church must operate according to sound business principles and structure.

Membership Tracking Systems

Membership tracking is not just another administrative function. It has its foundations in Jesus' parable of the lost sheep.

> Then drew near unto him all the publicans and sinners for to hear him. And the Pharisees and scribes murmured, saying, This man receiveth sinners, and eateth with them. And he spake this parable unto them, saying, What man of you, having an hundred sheep, if he lose one of them, doth not leave the ninety and nine in the wilderness, and go after that which is lost, until he find it? And when he hath found it, he layeth it on his shoulders, rejoicing. And when he cometh home, he calleth together his friends and neighbours, saying unto them, Rejoice with me; for I have found my sheep which was lost.
>
> Luke 15:1-6

When purchasing any church management software, make sure your integrity is in line and that you have proper motivation. Your software should not be used for personal business ventures. They have been designed to help churches do what is normally difficult to do manually; it is humanly impossible to keep a personal touch with each member of a growing progressive church without the proper technology. Long gone are the old church archive books and the church clerks. Church management software allows you to send personal letters and phone calls to every member from infants to adults.

The Data Administrator's office retrieves all of the written information and forms for financial contributions, attendance, membership records, participation and more. Statistical reports are maintained by the data office staff to be used for accessing the growth, strategic planning, grants, or bank requirements.

Administrative Procedures

All administrative processes, from financial to human resources, should be developed to structure the operations of the overall ministry. The administrative team should consist of the Business Operations Director, the Church Administrator, the Accountant, the Human Resource Director, the Data Administrator, and the Associate Pastors. With the vision and master plan clearly defined, this team should meet each week to access growth, make revisions and recommendations, and then package this report to be taken to the senior pastor who is the CEO. Other departmental leaders can be called into the meeting as needed. Each associate pastor residing over a department will provide written documentation of their departmental status to bring to the meeting. Establish a standard monthly reporting form for every department. (Samples of these forms are found in the resource book, *Building God's House Resource Book – 200 Pages of Power to Succeed in Ministry.* Refer to the Appendix for more information.)

Many senior pastors fail because they do not realize the importance of letting their staff manage the day to day details of ministry operations in order to free them to then handle the big issues, which is representing the overall ministry in city, state, and even national organizations. The weekly report package should include graphs and pictures to show new members profiles, financial reports, calendar and event issues, and project status. An old saying that is true defines insanity as doing the same thing "over and over" again in the same way but expecting different results. Selah

Your statistics help you to make adjustments to stop stagnant or slothful ministry operations.

Your charts should show the scales moving up. The moment you see the scales going down, you should immediately make changes to keep the stats up.

Restructuring the location of the administrative offices is another important process to enable the ministry to operate more smoothly. Have you ever heard the statement, "Time is money?" It doesn't make very much sense to position the office of the manager over a department away from where his team, his primary responsibility. The amount of time that it takes for that person to walk across campus or up or down ten floors could add up to dollars that could affect the operation of that department which would affect the total operation.

Frankly, the organizational flow chart is the tool that sets the structure for practically everything. The organizational flow chart should dictate the administrative filing system so that even when a staff person or leader leaves the ministry, the next person will be able to pick up immediately where the other person left.

Powerful Leadership Meetings — Celebrate Your Workforce!

Do you have boring leadership meetings? Do you have to coerce your leaders to attend? I think I probably have said it at least five times already in this book. And here it goes again.

People like to be involved in things that are exciting! People need to know that you appreciate what they do!

I absolutely know that church workers are some of the hardest working people in the world. They deserve ten thousand accolades.

1. Your leadership meetings should paint a picture to the leaders to spell out the status of the vision through power point presentations.

2. The meeting should begin with a fellowship time with refreshments and beautiful music to set an atmosphere of joy. Leaders rarely get the opportunity to just get to know each other. In a progressive, growing church, most of the leaders are always running from the moment they set foot on the campus until they leave.
3. If any leadership positions are changing or if new leaders are added, this is the time to make the introductions and announcements and to keep the organizational structure in tact. Create methods to provoke the leaders to mingle.
4. Impact the meeting, but keep it short. Get straight to the point! Value their time.
5. The Associate Pastors and the paid staff should serve the volunteers, because if they did not have the hundreds of volunteers for their support staff, they would not be able to produce the great things that they do for the ministry.
6. The themes of the leadership meetings should center on the holidays but always tie in with the vision.
7. Once a year, turn the leadership meeting into your annual meeting and open it for the church members to attend so that they can hear the administrative status of the ministry.

These sound organizational changes will draw professionals such as attorneys, teachers, doctors, and people from all walks of life that are searching for a place to bring their family for total edification. Because neither the denominational title nor race matters, your ministry will become a melting pot with people from all denominational backgrounds as well as ethnicities. Regardless of what anyone may say, people want to be involved in ministries where there is order and clearly defined directives (vision).

In 1989, Bishop R.K. Hash hired Dr. Harvey Watson to conduct workshops for getting the church business in order. Dr. Watson made the pastors realize the importance of having the church financial records structured to meet all of the IRS requirements for offerings, special services such as the Pastor's Anniversary, and the hiring processes according to the Department of Labor standards. His teachings provoked the pastors to realize that their ministries must run according to the laws of the land for all practices from sanitation, safety, immigration rules for the missionaries and students, and the use of all purchased equipment, automobiles, and supplies for ministry. Of course, many people did not understand these new rules. They felt that because they had paid their tithes to the church, they should be able to obtain a van or tables and chairs for their family reunions and birthday parties whenever they wanted to get them. They did not realize that by doing so would put the ministry in jeopardy and possibly lose their non-profit status. Also, they had to be taught that their tithes belonged to God and it was their personal obedience to His Word to bring their tithes to the storehouse. Tithes are not paid to the pastor nor for free favors.

The pastor is not a 501c3 organization. The government gives a tax-exempt status to organizations and churches. The church is an organization; therefore, the tithes are brought to the church, the storehouse, and the contributions must be recorded by the finance department to be able to give a statement at the end of the year to their members for a tax write-off.

I have assisted many pastors throughout the country and I have been amazed at how many of them do not use offering envelopes to keep records of the financial contributions. They are still just passing the bucket. There is no financial accountability or any basic administrative processes in place. Frankly, this is unfair to the members of the church. Legally they deserve to receive a contribution statement for tax purposes, but even more so as their spiritual leaders, pastors should demonstrate integrity by getting sound business processes in place.

Financial Systems and Accountability

The finance office must be equipped with proper software that accounts for every penny that comes into the ministry. Bishop Hash hired Gordon Slade, an accountant and life long friend of the family, to orchestrate the management of the finance office to meet all IRS standards. Our offering envelopes were even reformatted, because the offering envelope is a legal document that verifies that a contribution was made to a non-profit organization. The envelopes serve as a "check and balance" for the financial records and are kept on file for a minimum of five years. Scriptures for the promises of God concerning our giving was printed on the envelopes as a reminder to the people of our covenant with Him.

For control purposes, all financial transactions for the total ministry operations must be managed through the finance office. All procedures for purchase requests, credit cards, and departmental budgets and accounts should be passed down from this office. The counting room must be equipped with counting machines, a safe, and other necessary tools that equate to a bank system.

Because of teaching the congregation how to give as unto the Lord, the people no longer had to be coerced to give. During these changes at St. Peter's, Bishop Hash had the finance department purchase white offering utensils that looked like chitterling buckets, at least that is what the people laughed and called them. This is a typical thing that you see now, but it was strange at that time.

Church Public Relations

In the secular business world, we hear the terms "core" and "image." Likewise, the church must also establish its core and determine a significant image it desires to project to its community. Your core determines who you really are. What is it that your ministry does better than and different from all the other thousands of churches in the city? Of course, this too is taken from the vision. Once this is determined, you must package your core and image into everything that you print: bulletins, envelopes, stationery, newsletters, and so on. Your web page should project this image as well. Either hire a professional marketing company to package your ministry or you can set up a marketing department with the proper software to do it in-house.

Develop a good protocol system for the church. Every leader and volunteer worker should be trained in quality customer service. Professional voice tone and body language are skills that must be taught. People do not automatically have these qualities. Ushers and greeters are the first line team. Make sure they are properly trained to greet people and to make them feel welcome in your church. They should know where every class is from the children up to adults, because they also serve as direction givers. Again, like Timothy was to Paul, they are the ones who project the image of the senior pastor and his wife.

Communication Center

The communication center is a nucleus area for the hundreds of volunteers and staff that give their gifts and talents to the vision on a daily basis. This center maintains a mailbox system by which all of the church leaders receive notices and announcements, pictures of new volunteers are posted on bulletin boards, and other news is related. Most churches today are equipped with e-mail and communication software technology; however, forms, memos, bulletins, newsletters, bulletin boards, and phone tree systems are necessary methods to keep all of the leaders informed. This center also serves as a check in and checkout place where the workforce can pick up their badges and to get last minute details for services and events.

Placing each of the previously mentioned administrative processes sets a solid foundation for consistent church growth.

Make the Vision Clear. No Gimmicks, No Tricks!

Take all of your annual themes from the vision and project them in a way that everyone, from children to adults, can embrace.

1. Form a building fund committee to create a plan that gives the opportunity for every boy, girl, woman, and man to give *consistently according to their economical level.* You can look at materials from many professional fundraising companies. They are great companies, but no one knows your people like you do. If you tap into heart power, you will find the secret for fundraising. *The secret to their heart is to invest in them.*
2. Your marketing department can make simple brochures to mail to every membership household, distribute them in the bulletins, and place them in strategic places throughout the campus.
3. The arts department can write skits to present every first

Sunday. Mobilize the children, teens and adults in the skits.
4. A change offering can be started. Eventually the word will spread in the community. People who are not even members will begin to bring big jars of change that they have been saving to the church office. The children can start bringing their piggy banks to the church. This change can add up to be several hundred thousands of dollars.
5. A job bank can be formed that is supplied by the members. Many times companies do not publicly post their jobs. The members should be encouraged to look out for job openings at their places of employment and to bring the information to the job bank. *By making sure that all of the members are gainfully employed, they will be empowered to be consistent and faithful to their tithes and building fund vows as well as to take care of their families.*
6. Start a class to show the members how to do family budgeting and to get out of debt. Self-preservation has been and always will be first in people's lives. How can they be faithful to a building fund campaign, something that they cannot see, when their lights are about to go off, or when there is not enough food to feed their family?
7. Organize a business club to teach the members how to look within themselves to find their dominant gift to develop into a business. Soon, everyone will have business cards. This will boost the self-esteem of the people because their love to clean silver, cut grass, clean houses, wash cars, etc. will become a financial reservoir from God.

Invest in people and people will invest in the vision.

Profit Centers — The Associate Pastors as Executive Directors and Supervisors

Be kindly affectioned one to another with brotherly love; in honour preferring one another; *Not slothful in business;*

fervent in spirit; serving the Lord; Rejoicing in hope; patient in tribulation; continuing instant in prayer; Distributing to the necessity of saints; given to hospitality.
Romans 12:11

Seest thou a man diligent in his business? he shall stand before kings; he shall not stand before mean men.
Proverbs 22:29

Wherefore, brethren, look ye out among you seven men of honest report, full of the Holy Ghost and wisdom, whom we may *appoint over this business.*
Acts 6:3

Every associate pastor who has been placed over a department should develop his/her department to become a profit center. In the corporate world, the associate pastors would equate to executive directors or supervisors. Executive directors and supervisors are responsible for making a profit for the company. And when they don't, they get fired because it is unfair to the owner of the company to carry dead weight that could potentially cause his company to go bankrupt. Associate pastors must know when to be spiritual as well as how to be practical businessmen and women. They should be aware of various funding sources that are available for their departments and make their own budgets if possible.

Scenario: Everything at the mall is spread out for customers to spend, spend, and spend. The store managers are skilled at how to make their products appealing to the senses of the customers through colorful displays, lighting, music, temperature, and smell of the room, etc. The members who come to your church and the people in the community are your customers. They patronize your bookstore, your before and after school programs for children and youth, your men and women's organizations, your cafeteria, your senior home, etc. In the same way that the shopping mall store managers make their products appealing to their customers, the associate pastors must do the same.

The twenty-first century church is a place that serves the total family seven days a week, not just on Sunday and Wednesday.

In the past, most church buildings were only used on Sundays and Wednesdays. Since the building is being paid for three hundred and sixty-five days a year, why not maximize the use of your facilities each of those days? Why have large auditoriums that are only used on Sunday mornings when they can become conference centers and earn profits by renting them out for community events? Join the city chamber of commerce and place your facilities on the convention and visitor's bureau listing.

The associate pastor residing over the Facilities Management department must make sure that all legalities are in place, and let your facilities become profit centers. Establish a complete business plan of operations. You can staff the events either through your Ministry of Helps office or through temporary agencies. This, too, is a way to bridge your church with your community. People who come to the events also find out about your church and all of the other programs that you offer for total family enrichment. Your Christian creed will dictate what type of events you approve to be held in your facilities.

There are no shortages in God's house.

The Capital Fund Raising Department

Isaiah 6:3 states that the whole earth is filled with His glory and Psalms 24:1-2 declares that the earth is the Lord's and the fullness thereof. Every diamond and every ounce of gold that God created is still on this earth. In spite of what the media says, there are no shortages on earth. Doesn't it make sense that God, the Creator of the earth, would make provisions for His own company? Tithes, offerings, pledges, and vows are only a part of the methods used to finance the vision of God.

The capital fund raising team serves as a financial and administrative liaison between the church departments and funding sources.

This team makes sure that the non-profit funds from corporations, foundations, and other donors and sponsors are carried out in accordance with the state and federal laws. They maintain a data bank of funding sources such as corporations, foundations, donors, and sponsors and work indirectly with the accounting department.

The capital fund raising team should join any of the many national fundraising organizations, because these organizations not only give training in grant writing, they also provide information for current funding sources.

This team orchestrates the opportunity for members to establish wills, trusts, and other methods of financial contributions. Their loyalty to their church can continue even when they have left earth to go to heaven. They leave a legacy for the next generation.

For some reason, people think that a non-profit organization cannot make a profit and that it should be poor. Nonsense! It takes money to fulfill a big vision. Non-profits can make as much money as for-profits. The main difference is that with a non-profit organization, all profits are owned by and must be used for the non-profit organization, and not for personal gain.

The Business Owners in the Church

Many times business owners look for non-profit organizations to adopt for tax purposes. Your church or any of your ministry departments can be that organization if you have a 501c3 tax-exempt status. The business owners will often contribute their business expertise or make contributions of furniture, computers, and other products and services.

All gifts are in the house. If your members believe in the vision and believe in their pastor, and when you have your business structure in tact, they will tithe not only from their personal salaries, but they will tithe from their business profits as well. The same spiritual blessing applies in both instances.

Community Enhancement Services

Many of the things that God puts in the heart of the pastor are really community service programs. These programs should operate under a separate 501c3 from that of the church. With a thorough business plan, the community programs, such as a day care, senior care, youth and children's programs, qualify for corporate, private, and government funding.

Do not expect the tithes and offerings to finance the total vision when there are so many other financial means that God has placed on this earth for the church to tap into. Become wise in business.

The Power of Recognition and Appreciation

The offerings are celebration ceremonies to give the congregation an opportunity to praise God for their blessings. Each Sunday, members and families should have the opportunity to bring their sacrificial offerings and gifts to God, not the pastor. When a need arises in the church, make it known to the congregation through the bulletin or newsletter. Many times God will move upon the heart of a member, family, or business owner in the audience to meet the need. When people understand the principle of seedtime and harvest, pastors will not have to beg them to give. They will know that giving to God is another form of worship.

Immediate gratification is a human trait that we all possess. When we do something good, we want someone to recognize our effort and give us a pat on the shoulder. We all need and love affirmation; therefore, your finance office should send a personalized letter from the senior pastor to the contributors. The phone tree system can be used to give a personal message of thanks to everyone each week. In order to keep up the momentum and spirit of giving going, you must stay connected to your contributors weekly, monthly, quarterly, and annually. Don't just wait until the end of the year.

> Then was our mouth filled with laughter, and our tongue with singing: then said they among the heathen, The Lord hath done great things for them. The Lord hath done great things for us, whereof we are glad.
> Psalms 126:2-3

> Therefore with joy shall ye draw water out of the wells of salvation. And in that day shall ye say, Praise the Lord, call upon his name, declare his doings among the people, make

mention that his name is exalted. Sing unto the Lord; for he hath done excellent things: this is known in all the earth. Cry out and shout, thou inhabitant of Zion: for great is the Holy One of Israel in the midst of thee.

Isaiah 12:3-6

Surely, God would use His own company, (the Church), to be an example to the world.

CHAPTER FOUR

Strategy Four

Mobilize Your Church to Pray "Power for the Vision"

*"Establishing the Foundation:
The Church was Born out of Prayer"*

Establishing the Foundation:
The Church was Born out of Prayer.

Prayer is the key to see the things of the Spirit manifested in the natural. Knowing this, then every aspect of the operations of the ministry must be birthed and watered with fervent prayer. The Bible says that the prayers of a righteous man avails much.

How to Mobilize the Whole Church to Pray

The Bible gives us directions for how to pray and compels us to pray without ceasing.

> Now we exhort you, brethren, warn them that are unruly, comfort the feebleminded, support the weak, be patient toward all men. See that none render evil for evil unto any

man; but ever follow that which is good, both among yourselves, and to all men. Rejoice evermore. *Pray without ceasing. In every thing give thanks: for this is the will of God in Christ Jesus concerning you.*

I Thessalonians 5:14-18

Just as Jesus taught the disciples to pray, we must teach the body of Christ to pray:

Take heed that ye do not your alms before men, to be seen of them: otherwise ye have no reward of your Father which is in heaven. Therefore when thou doest thine alms, do not sound a trumpet before thee, as the hypocrites do in the synagogues and in the streets, that they may have glory of men. Verily I say unto you, They have their reward. But when thou doest alms, let not thy left hand know what thy right hand doeth: That thine alms may be in secret: and thy Father which seeth in secret himself shall reward thee openly. *And when thou prayest, thou shalt not be as the hypocrites are: for they love to pray standing in the synagogues and in the corners of the streets, that they may be seen of men.* Verily I say unto you, They have their reward. *But thou, when thou prayest, enter into thy closet, and when thou hast shut thy door, pray to thy Father which is in secret; and thy Father which seeth in secret shall reward thee openly.*

But when ye pray, use not vain repetitions, as the heathen do: for they think that they shall be heard for their much speaking. Be not ye therefore like unto them: for your Father knoweth what things ye have need of, before ye ask him. After this manner therefore pray ye: Our Father which art in heaven, Hallowed be thy name. Thy kingdom come, Thy will be done in earth, as it is in heaven. Give us this day our daily bread. And forgive us our debts, as we forgive our debtors.

Matthew 6:1-13

Repeatedly, the scriptures instruct us to always pray. As we wrap our lives with the Spirit of God and converse with the heavenlies, then God's spiritual promises will manifest in the natural.

Begin everything with prayer or a prayerful attitude. Keep God involved.

In the beginning God created the heaven and the earth. And the earth was without form, and void; and darkness was upon the face of the deep. And the Spirit of God moved upon the face of the waters. *And God said*, Let there be light: and there was light. *And God saw* the light, that it was good: and God divided the light from the darkness. *And God called* the light Day, and the darkness he called Night. And the evening and the morning were the first day.

And God said, Let there be a firmament in the midst of the waters, and let it divide the waters from the waters. *And God made* the firmament, and divided the waters which were under the firmament from the waters which were above the firmament: and it was so. *And God called* the firmament Heaven. And the evening and the morning were the second day.

And God said, Let the waters under the heaven be gathered together unto one place, and let the dry land appear: and it was so. *And God called* the dry land Earth; and the gathering together of the waters called he Seas: *and God saw* that it was good. *And God said*, Let the earth bring forth grass, the herb yielding seed, and the fruit tree yielding fruit after his kind, whose seed is in itself, upon the earth: and it was so. And the earth brought forth grass, and herb yielding seed after his kind, and the tree yielding fruit, whose seed was in itself, after his kind: *and God saw* that it was good. And the evening and the morning were the third day.

And God said, Let there be lights in the firmament of the heaven to divide the day from the night; and let them be for signs, and for seasons, and for days, and years: And let them be for lights in the firmament of the heaven to give light upon the earth: and it was so. *And God made* two great lights; the greater light to rule the day, and the lesser light to rule the night: he made the stars also. *And God set* them in the firmament of the heaven to give light upon the earth, And to rule over the day and over the night, and to divide the light from the darkness: *and God saw* that it was good. And the evening and the morning were the fourth day.

And God said, Let the waters bring forth abundantly the moving creature that hath life, and fowl that may fly above the earth in the open firmament of heaven. *And God created* great whales, and every living creature that moveth, which the waters brought forth abundantly, after their kind, and every winged fowl after his kind: *and God saw* that it was good. *And God blessed* them, saying, Be fruitful, and multiply, and fill the waters in the seas, and let fowl multiply in the earth. And the evening and the morning were the fifth day. *And God said,* Let the earth bring forth the living creature after his kind, cattle, and creeping thing, and beast of the earth after his kind: and it was so. *And God made* the beast of the earth after his kind, and cattle after their kind, and every thing that creepeth upon the earth after his kind: *and God saw* that it was good.

And God said, Let us make man in our image, after our likeness: and let them have dominion over the fish of the sea, and over the fowl of the air, and over the cattle, and over all the earth, and over every creeping thing that creepeth upon the earth.

So God created man in his own image, in the image of God created he him; male and female created he them. And God blessed them, and God said unto them, Be fruitful, and multiply, and replenish the earth, and subdue it: and have dominion over the fish of the sea, and over the fowl of the air, and over every living thing that moveth upon the earth.

And God said, Behold, I have given you every herb bearing seed, which is upon the face of all the earth, and every tree, in the which is the fruit of a tree yielding seed; to you it shall be for meat. And to every beast of the earth, and to every fowl of the air, and to every thing that creepeth upon the earth, wherein there is life, I have given every green herb for meat: and it was so.

And God saw every thing that he had made, and, behold, it was very good. And the evening and the morning were the sixth day.

Genesis 1

The principle here is that God uses Himself to illustrate to us how we should begin everything we do in His name in order to subdue all that He has given us on earth.

Thus the heavens and the earth were finished, and all the host of them. And on the seventh day *God ended his work* which he had made; and he rested on the seventh day from all his work which he had made. *And God blessed* the seventh day, and sanctified it: because that in it he had rested from all his work which God created and made. These are the generations of the heavens and of the earth when they were created, in the day that the LORD God made the earth and the heavens, And every plant of the field before it was in the earth, and every herb of the field before it grew: for the LORD God had not caused it to rain upon the earth, and there was not a man to till the ground. But there went up a mist from the earth, and watered the whole face of the ground. And the LORD God formed man of the dust of the ground, and breathed into his nostrils the breath of life; and man became a living soul.

And the LORD God planted a garden eastward in Eden; and there he put the man whom he had formed. And out of the ground made the LORD God to grow every tree that is pleasant to the sight, and good for food; the tree of life also in the midst of the garden, and the tree of knowledge of good and evil. And a river went out of Eden to water the garden; and from thence it was parted, and became into four heads. The name of the first is Pison: that is it which compasseth the whole land of Havilah, where there is gold; And the gold of that land is good: there is bdellium and the onyx stone. And the name of the second river is Gihon: the same is it that compasseth the whole land of Ethiopia. And the name of the third river is Hiddekel: that is it which goeth toward the east of Assyria. And the fourth river is Euphrates.

And the LORD God took the man, and put him into the garden of Eden to dress it and to keep it. *And the LORD God commanded* the man, saying, Of every tree of the garden thou mayest freely eat: But of the tree of the knowledge of good and evil, thou shalt not eat of it: for in the day that thou eatest thereof thou shalt surely die. *And the LORD God said*, It is not good that the man should be alone; I will make him an help meet for him. And out of the ground the LORD God formed every beast of the field, and every fowl of the air; and brought them unto Adam to see what he would call them: and whatsoever Adam called every living creature, that was the name thereof. And Adam gave names to all cattle, and to the fowl of the air, and to every beast of the field; but for Adam there was not found an help meet for him.

And the LORD God caused a deep sleep to fall upon Adam, and he slept: and he took one of his ribs, and closed up the flesh instead thereof; And the rib, which the LORD God had taken from man, made he a woman, and brought her unto

the man. And Adam said, This is now bone of my bones, and flesh of my flesh: she shall be called Woman, because she was taken out of Man. Therefore shall a man leave his father and his mother, and shall cleave unto his wife: and they shall be one flesh. And they were both naked, the man and his wife, and were not ashamed
Genesis 2

For your reference, please read the following scriptures:

Psalms 122:6	Pray for the peace of Jerusalem
Matthew 5:44	Pray for them which despitefully use you and persecute you
James 5:13-15	Pray for the sick and afflicted and one for the other
James 5:16	The effectual fervent prayer of a righteous man avails much
Ephesians 6:18	Praying always with all prayer and supplication in the Spirit and watching thereunto with all perseverance and supplication for all saints;
I Timothy 2:1-2	Pray for all men, kings, and for all that are in authority
Philippians 4:6	By prayer and supplication with thanksgiving let your requests be made known unto God
I John 5:14-15	And this is the confidence that we have in him, that, if we ask any thing according to his will, he heareth us: And if we know that he hear us, whatsoever we ask, we know that we have the petitions that we desired of him.

Make clear prayer agendas for the children, youth, and adults. Include the following in your prayer agenda list:
- pastor and leaders
- needs of the church

- needs of the people
- pastors throughout the city and the world
- local, national, and international leaders

The total church should pray and speak the same things and move in the same direction. Because the attention is focused on teaching the people how to achieve the things of God, any division should be removed. And as a result of the people's dedication, supernatural financial blessings come to the church.

As families arrive at church together, they may go to separate facilities; however, the same message should be taught on every level. As the families drive home together, each family member can contribute to the conversation from their level. A specific week of each month can be designated for total family worship and prayer whereby everyone will stay in the main auditorium. The reason for this strategy is twofold: the children are able to see examples of prayer and worship in their parents and entire families are able to sit together in the worship service.

The Value of the Senior Members

The elders which are among you I exhort, who am also an elder, and a witness of the sufferings of Christ, and also a partaker of the glory that shall be revealed: Feed the flock of God which is among you, taking the oversight thereof, not by constraint, but willingly; not for filthy lucre, but of a ready mind; Neither as being lords over God's heritage, but being ensamples to the flock. And when the chief Shepherd shall appear, ye shall receive a crown of glory that fadeth not away.

Likewise, ye younger, submit yourselves unto the elder. Yea, all of you be subject one to another, and be clothed with humility: for God resisteth the proud, and giveth grace to the humble. Humble yourselves therefore under the mighty hand of God, that he may exalt you in due time...

I Peter 5:1-6

Mildred T. Hash Mother's Board

One of the strongest organizations in the church at St. Peter's World Outreach Center is the Mildred T. Hash Mother's Board, which consists of all of the senior ladies of the church that are 65 years old and older. The board

- teams up with the prayer director and keeps a prayer covering over the vision at all times,
- conducts the noonday prayer services, and
- helps in the nursery to rock the babies to sleep.

The Sensational Seniors Fellowship

The Sensational Seniors Fellowship consists of both male and female senior members who have monthly fellowship outings. Reserved parking and seating is held for these elite people for all services. A team is in place to make sure that the senior members do not get lost in the midst of the phenomenal growth that the ministry is experiencing. Likewise, they stay connected to the seniors to make sure their needs are met in the cold winters and hot summer months. This team conducts workshops on topics such as how to enjoy their senior years, finances, health, and more.

So much attention is given to this segment of people because they are pillars of the church. They have stood by the vision long before the new people came. They were pioneers and paved the way for the wonderful fruit that everyone is enjoying today, and so they have earned the right to receive red carpet respect.

> That the aged men be sober, grave, temperate, sound in faith, in charity, in patience. The aged women likewise, that they be in behaviour as becometh holiness, not false accusers, not given to much wine, teachers of good things; *That they may teach the young women to be sober, to love their husbands, to love their children, To be discreet, chaste, keepers at home, good, obedient to their own husbands, that the Word of God be not blasphemed.*

> Young men likewise exhort to be sober minded. *In all things shewing thyself a pattern of good works: in doctrine shewing*

uncorruptness, gravity, sincerity, Sound speech, that cannot be condemned; that he that is of the contrary part may be ashamed, having no evil thing to say of you.

Titus 2:2-8

Rebuke not an elder, but intreat him as a father; and the younger men as brethren; The elder women as mothers; the younger as sisters, with all purity.

I Timothy 5:1-2

Bishop Hash's Strategy for Prayer

One of the errors that most pastors make is to try to clone everyone to fit into one glove. Yes, personal and corporate prayer is necessary, but when schedules demand that people neglect their families, jobs, and careers in order to pray, their lives are prone to becoming unbalanced. If possible, find a place on your campus that can be kept open for an open prayer chapel. This way, people can come and go at their own leisure.

Another way to successfully motivate the whole church to pray is to assign teams of leaders to conduct prayer sessions three times a day: morning, noon, and evening. Make these sessions available to the public and leaders so they can choose which session they desire to attend. No one's lifestyle is the same everyday.

The Power of Prayer Class

Develop a prayer class to be held during the regular School of Ministry hour on Sundays. Here are some suggested topics:

1. The Word of God and Prayer
2. The Name of Jesus and Prayer
3. The Blood of Jesus and Prayer
4. The Holy Spirit and Prayer
5. Love and Sensitivity of Heart
6. Prayer and Fasting
7. Praying To Get Results
8. Prayer of Faith
9. Prayer of Agreement

10. Prayer of Consecration and Commitment
11. Prayer of Intercession and Supplication
12. Prayer of Thanks, Praise, and Worship

Midnight and All Night Prayer Vigils

In order to have all of the leaders and staff praying together, conduct a midnight prayer and even an all-night prayer vigil. The key to leadership prayer is to create a win-win situation for everyone involved. This eliminates the frustration of trying to get everyone to pray together at the same time. It's not that they do not want to pray. The problem may be that they have other obligations and responsibilities outside of the church that places a demand on their time. Flexibility is a vital key to successful ministry.

National Prayer Ministry Staffing

Companies have evolved over the years that offer management services for a national prayer ministry whereby people from around the world can call in twenty-four hours a day. These companies are wonderful because they have trained people ready and available, give a complete data report of the demographics of the callers, and protect the integrity of the ministry. I caution pastors not to try to have twenty-four hour national prayer ministries using volunteers. Oftentimes they will start off on fire until reality kicks in. It gets harder and harder to get out of bed at 5:00 AM or to serve their volunteer hours at three o'clock in the morning, and the integrity of your call-in prayer ministry is damaged.

Community Prayer and Fasting Day

I once developed a concept for one of my clients called Community Prayer and Fasting Day. It was held each week whereby we invited city officials, school board administrators, or other community agencies to speak and bring their prayer requests. This was another method to bridge the gap between the church and the community. We share the same vision as the city: to make a better place for our families to live.

The purpose of the community prayer is to build relationships with the city leaders. Because the mayor's desire for the city is to increase the lives of the people, the pastor and the mayor may share the same vision: to build the people. If our nation is really built on "In God We Trust," then we should collaborate with our community, state, and local authorities to address their concerns for developing the citizens, which are the people in our pews.

Embrace the National Day of Prayer Community Events. During the National Day of Prayer, your church should team up with the citywide events and offer assistance and involvement through collaborative efforts.

Help your leaders be committed by placing importance on the things they are involved in and as a result, they will be loyal and embrace the prayer ministry, the finances of the church, and the overall vision.

As a result of establishing a fervent, consistent, and well-structured prayer covering over the entire ministry and the congregation, many signs and wonders occurred at St. Peter's. My brother, J.C., started a healing school class at the Highland Street church that was held every Tuesday and Thursday. One day when the instructor, Mr. Roberts, was teaching, he looked up in the ceiling and saw beams of fire blazing, but there was no smell of smoke. Everyone immediately was ushered out of the church and a call was made to the fire station. When the fire marshal arrived, he went up into the attic to see where the fire was coming from and saw the blazes himself, but, when the fire truck arrived, there was no longer a fire, no sign of smoke, and not even any burn stains. Of course, this puzzled the fire marshal. After all, he called for the big fire truck to come. It was noted in the documented report that there *appeared* to be a fire, but that sunrays must have caused it . There are no windows in the attic, so there could not have been any sunrays blazing.

At another service held in the Phase One building, the power of God was so thick that people were "slain in the spirit" all over the church. One of the choir members saw musical notes floating in the air and took a picture of them.

Many other miraculous things happened beyond human explanation because of tapping into the Spirit of the living God through P-R-A-Y-E-R. The picture and the fire marshal's report are still on file at St. Peter's as documented proof of the power of God.

CHAPTER FIVE

Strategy Five

Evangelize for Church Growth

"Accepting the Call to Evangelize and to Mobilize Every Member for Evangelism"

Lifestyle Evangelism - Accept the Call to Evangelize and Mobilize Every Member for Evangelism.

Repeatedly, the Bible instructs us to win souls, tell the multitudes about the life of Christ, and teach people how to live, move, and have their being in Christ.

The bottom line of our business is to win souls!

The fruit of the righteous is a tree of life; and he that winneth souls is wise.

Proverbs 11:30

And Jesus went about all the cities and villages, teaching in their synagogues, and preaching the gospel of the kingdom, and healing every sickness and every disease among the

people. But when he saw the multitudes, he was moved with compassion on them, because they fainted, and were scattered abroad, as sheep having no shepherd. Then saith he unto his disciples, *The harvest truly is plenteous, but the labourers are few; Pray ye therefore the Lord of the harvest, that he will send forth labourers into his harvest.*
Matthew 9:35-38

But go rather to the lost sheep of the house of Israel. And as ye go, preach, saying, The kingdom of heaven is at hand.
Matthew 10:6-7

And Jesus, walking by the sea of Galilee, saw two brethren, Simon called Peter, and Andrew his brother, casting a net into the sea: for they were fishers. And he saith unto them, Follow me, and I will make you fishers of men. And they straightway left their nets, and followed him. And going on from thence, he saw other two brethren, James the son of Zebedee, and John his brother, in a ship with Zebedee their father, mending their nets; and he called them. And they immediately left the ship and their father, and followed him. *And Jesus went about all Galilee, teaching in their synagogues, and preaching the gospel of the kingdom, and healing all manner of sickness and all manner of disease among the people.*

And his fame went throughout all Syria: and they brought unto him all sick people that were taken with divers diseases and torments, and those which were possessed with devils, and those which were lunatick, and those that had the palsy; and he healed them. *And there followed him great multitudes of people from Galilee, and from Decapolis, and from Jerusalem, and from Judaea, and from beyond Jordan.*
Matthew 4:18-22

And Jesus said unto them, Come ye after me, and I will make you to become *fishers of men.*
Mark 1:17

And Jesus answering said unto them, They that are whole need not a physician; but they that are sick. I came not to call the righteous, but sinners to repentance.
                                    Luke 5:31-32

That it might be fulfilled which was spoken by Esaias the prophet, saying, himself took our infirmities, and bare our sicknesses. Now when Jesus saw great multitudes about him, he gave commandment to depart unto the other side. And a certain scribe came, and said unto him, Master, I will follow thee whithersoever thou goest
                                    Matthew 8:17-19

For the Son of man is not come to destroy men's lives, but to save them. And they went to another village. And it came to pass, that, as they went in the way, a certain man said unto him, Lord, I will follow thee whithersoever thou goest.

And Jesus came and spake unto them, saying, All power is given unto me in heaven and in earth. *Go ye therefore, and teach all nations, baptizing them in the name of the Father, and of the Son, and of the Holy Ghost*: Teaching them to observe all things whatsoever I have commanded you: and, lo, I am with you alway, even unto the end of the world. Amen.
                                    Luke 9:56-57

Who will have all men to be saved, and to come unto the knowledge of the truth. For there is one God, and one mediator between God and men, the man Christ Jesus; Who gave himself a ransom for all, to be testified in due time.
                                    I Timothy 2:4-6

Take heed that ye despise not one of these little ones; for I say unto you, That in heaven their angels do always behold the face of my Father which is in heaven. For the Son of man is come to save that which was lost. How think ye? if a man have an hundred sheep, and one of them be gone astray, doth he not leave the ninety and nine, and goeth into the mountains, and seeketh that which is gone astray? And if so be that he find it, verily I say unto you, *he rejoiceth more of that sheep, than of the ninety and nine which went not astray. Even so it is not the will of your Father which is in heaven, that one of these little ones should perish.*

Matthew 18:10-14

Then drew near unto him all the publicans and sinners for to hear him. And the Pharisees and scribes murmured, saying, This man receiveth sinners, and eateth with them. And he spake this parable unto them, saying, What man of you, having an hundred sheep, if he lose one of them, doth not leave the ninety and nine in the wilderness, and go after that which is lost, until he find it? And when he hath found it, he layeth it on his shoulders, rejoicing. *And when he cometh home, he calleth together his friends and neighbours, saying unto them, Rejoice with me; for I have found my sheep which was lost. I say unto you, that likewise joy shall be in heaven over one sinner that repenteth, more than over ninety and nine just persons, which need no repentance.*

Luke 15:1-7

The church should be a spiritual healing center. After all, isn't that why Jesus died on the cross? Don't you think God knew that man would make a mess out of things here on earth? No matter what a person looks like on the outside, their spirit may be torn and broken on the inside. Thus, what we end up with is confusion and pain. The Bible tells us not to be ignorant of the devil's devices, so knowing this we must be wise and have a strategy to combat this plague and turn things around into the direction that God has predestined for His people. The church must teach about how personality disorders and ungodly character behavior evolve in a person's life. *As Christians, we should possess the character of God.*

This I say then, Walk in the Spirit, and ye shall not fulfil the lust of the flesh. For the flesh lusteth against the Spirit, and the Spirit against the flesh: and these are contrary the one to the other: so that ye cannot do the things that ye would. But if ye be led of the Spirit, ye are not under the law. Now the works of the flesh are manifest, which are these; Adultery, fornication, uncleanness, lasciviousness, Idolatry, witchcraft, hatred, variance, emulations, wrath, strife, seditions, heresies, Envyings, murders, drunkenness, revellings, and such like: of the which I tell you before, as I have also told you in time past, that they which do such things shall not inherit the kingdom of God. *But the fruit of the Spirit is love, joy, peace, longsuffering, gentleness, goodness, faith, Meekness, temperance: against such there is no law. And they that are Christ's have crucified the flesh with the affections and lusts. If we live in the Spirit, let us also walk in the Spirit. Let us not be desirous of vain glory, provoking one another, envying one another.*

Galatians 5:16-26

Are you aware that we store the memory of everything that we have smelled, touched, seen, heard, and tasted in our subconscious mind? How do you think a 40-year-old person can be hypnotized and yet respond like a two year old? Why is it that you wake up and are depressed for no apparent reason? What happened in your dreams or subconscious while you were asleep? You don't consciously know the reason why, but you are just depressed or you are happy. Or what happens when you hear a song that causes you to feel a certain way? What happens when you see a picture and it brings out certain feelings that you can't explain? Outward reactions are a direct result of inner emotions. Being timid, shy, full of fear, and short fused is not a part of the fruit of the spirit according to Galatians 5:22.

Generational Curses and Generational Blessings

As you read this wonderful passage from Deuteronomy 28, stop in between the verses and rejoice in knowing that our Father, God has taken care of everything for His children. Give Him honor and glory, knowing with assurance that the generational curses on your family no longer can prevail, because God has paid the price for our generational inheritance. Rejoice!

> *And it shall come to pass, if thou shalt hearken diligently unto the voice of the LORD thy God, to observe and to do all his commandments which I command thee this day, that the LORD thy God will set thee on high above all nations of the earth: And all these blessings shall come on thee, and overtake thee, if thou shalt hearken unto the voice of the LORD thy God.*

[Rejoice!]

Blessed shalt thou be in the city, and blessed shalt thou be in the field. *Blessed* shall be the fruit of thy body, and the fruit of thy ground, and the fruit of thy cattle, the increase of thy kine, and the flocks of thy sheep. *Blessed* shall be thy basket and thy store. *Blessed* shalt thou be when thou comest in, and blessed shalt thou be when thou goest *out*. The LORD shall cause thine enemies that rise up against thee to be smitten before thy face: they shall come out against thee one way, and flee before thee seven ways.

[Rejoice!]

The LORD shall command the blessing upon thee in thy storehouses, and in all that thou settest thine hand unto; and he shall *bless thee in the land which the LORD thy God giveth thee*. The LORD shall *establish thee an holy people unto himself,* as he hath sworn unto thee, if thou shalt keep the commandments of the LORD thy God, and walk in his ways.

[Rejoice!]

And all people of the earth shall see that thou art called by the name of the LORD; and they shall be afraid of thee. *And the LORD shall make thee plenteous in goods, in the fruit of thy body, and in the fruit of thy cattle, and in the fruit of thy ground, in the land which the LORD sware unto thy fathers to give thee. The LORD shall open unto thee his good treasure, the heaven to give the rain unto thy land in his season, and to bless all the work of thine hand: and thou shalt lend unto many nations, and thou shalt not borrow.*

[Rejoice!]

And the LORD *shall make thee the head, and not the tail; and thou shalt be above only, and thou shalt not be beneath*; if that thou hearken unto the commandments of the LORD thy God, which I command thee this day, to observe and to do them:

And thou shalt not go aside from any of the words which I command thee this day, to the right hand, or to the left, to go after other gods to serve them. But it shall come to pass, *if thou wilt not hearken unto the voice of the LORD thy God, to observe to do all his commandments and his statutes which I command thee this day; that all these curses shall come upon thee, and overtake thee: [Rejoice! That you have been warned!]*

We shouldn't stop rejoicing throughout the rest of the passage, but we should rejoice even more. Now we can understand why we have had so many attacks and devilish interruptions that have tried to discourage us and stop us from receiving the sure blessings that God sent His Son, Jesus on the cross to give to us.

Cursed shalt thou be in the city, and cursed shalt thou be in the field. Cursed shall be thy basket and thy store. Cursed shall be the fruit of thy body, and the fruit of thy land, the increase of thy kine, and the flocks of thy sheep. Cursed shalt thou be when thou comest in, and cursed shalt thou be when thou goest out. The LORD shall send upon thee cursing, vexation, and rebuke, in all that thou settest thine hand unto for to do, until thou be destroyed, and until thou perish quickly; because of the wickedness of thy doings, whereby thou hast forsaken me.

[Rejoice that you have been forgiven!]

The LORD shall make the pestilence cleave unto thee, until he have consumed thee from off the land, whither thou goest to possess it. The LORD shall smite thee with a consumption, and with a fever, and with an inflammation, and with an extreme burning, and with the sword, and with blasting, and with mildew; and they shall pursue thee until thou perish. And thy heaven that is over thy head shall be brass, and the earth that is under thee shall be iron. The LORD shall make the rain of thy land powder and dust: from heaven shall it come down upon thee, until thou be destroyed. The LORD shall cause thee to be smitten before thine enemies: thou shalt go out one way against them, and flee seven ways before them: and shalt be removed into all the kingdoms of the earth. And thy carcase shall be meat unto all fowls of the air, and unto the beasts of the earth, and no man shall fray them away. The LORD will smite thee with the botch of Egypt, and with the emerods, and with the scab, and with the itch, whereof thou canst not be healed.

[Rejoice that you have divine healing!]

The LORD shall smite thee with madness, and blindness, and astonishment of heart: And thou shalt grope at noonday, as the blind gropeth in darkness, and thou shalt not prosper in thy ways: and thou shalt be only oppressed and spoiled evermore, and no man shall save thee. Thou shalt betroth a wife, and another man shall lie with her: thou shalt build an house, and thou shalt not dwell therein: thou shalt plant a vineyard, and shalt not gather the grapes thereof. Thine ox shall be slain before thine eyes, and thou shalt not eat thereof: thine ass shall be violently taken away from before thy face, and shall not be restored to thee: thy sheep shall be given unto thine enemies, and thou shalt have none to rescue them.

[Rejoice that you have been redeemed!]

Thy sons and thy daughters shall be given unto another people, and thine eyes shall look, and fail with longing for them all the day long; and there shall be no might in thine hand. The fruit of thy land, and all thy labours, shall a nation which thou knowest not eat up; and thou shalt be only oppressed and crushed alway: So that thou shalt be mad for the sight of thine eyes which thou shalt see. The LORD shall smite thee in the knees, and in the legs, with a sore botch that cannot be healed, from the sole of thy foot unto the top of thy head. The LORD shall bring thee, and thy king which thou shalt set over thee, unto a nation which neither thou nor thy fathers have known; and there shalt thou serve other gods, wood and stone.

[Rejoice for the protection of your family!]

And thou shalt become an astonishment, a proverb, and a byword, among all nations whither the LORD shall lead thee. Thou shalt carry much seed out into the field, and shalt gather but little in; for the locust shall consume it. Thou shalt plant vineyards, and dress them, but shalt neither drink of the wine, nor gather the grapes; for the worms shall eat them. Thou shalt have olive trees throughout all thy coasts, but thou shalt not anoint thyself with the oil; for thine olive shall cast his fruit. Thou shalt beget sons and daughters, but thou shalt not enjoy them; for they shall go into captivity. All thy trees and fruit of thy land shall the locust consume.

The stranger that is within thee shall get up above thee very high; and thou shalt come down very low. He shall lend to thee, and thou shalt not lend to him: he shall be the head, and thou shalt be the tail.

[Rejoice that God has made you a great prosperous people!]

Moreover all these curses shall come upon thee, and shall pursue thee, and overtake thee, till thou be destroyed; because thou hearkenedst not unto the voice of the LORD thy God, to keep his commandments and his statutes which he commanded thee: And they shall be upon thee for a sign and for a wonder, and upon thy seed for ever. Because thou servedst not the LORD thy God with joyfulness, and with gladness of heart, for the abundance of all things; Therefore shalt thou serve thine enemies which the LORD shall send against thee, in hunger, and in thirst, and in nakedness, and in want of all things: and he shall put a yoke of iron upon thy neck, until he have destroyed thee. The LORD shall bring a nation against thee from far, from the end of the earth, as swift as the eagle flieth; a nation whose tongue thou shalt not understand; A nation of fierce countenance, which shall not regard the person of the old, nor shew favour to the young:

[Rejoice that God has given you power over your enemies!]

And he shall eat the fruit of thy cattle, and the fruit of thy land, until thou be destroyed: which also shall not leave thee either corn, wine, or oil, or the increase of thy kine, or flocks of thy sheep, until he have destroyed thee. And he shall besiege thee in all thy gates, until thy high and fenced walls come down, wherein thou trustedst, throughout all thy land: and he shall besiege thee in all thy gates throughout all thy land, which the LORD thy God hath given thee. And thou shalt eat the fruit of thine own body, the flesh of thy sons and of thy daughters, which the LORD thy God hath given thee, in the siege, and in the straitness, wherewith thine enemies shall distress thee: So that the man that is tender among you, and very delicate, his eye shall be evil toward his brother, and toward the wife of his bosom, and toward the remnant of his children which he shall leave: So that he will not give to any of them of the flesh of his children whom he shall eat: because he hath nothing left him in the siege, and in the straitness, wherewith thine enemies shall distress thee in all thy gates.

[Rejoice that you have been redeemed from the curse of the law!]

The tender and delicate woman among you, which would not adventure to set the sole of her foot upon the ground for delicateness and tenderness, her eye shall be evil toward the husband of her bosom, and toward her son, and toward her daughter, And toward her young one that cometh out from between her feet, and toward her children which she shall bear: for she shall eat them for want of all things secretly in the siege and straitness, wherewith thine enemy shall distress thee in thy gates. If thou wilt not observe to do all the words of this law that are written in this book, that thou mayest fear this glorious and fearful name, THE LORD THY GOD; Then the LORD will make thy plagues wonderful, and the plagues of thy seed, even great plagues, and of long continuance, and sore sicknesses, and of long continuance. Moreover he will bring upon thee all the diseases of Egypt, which thou wast afraid of; and they shall cleave unto thee. Also every sickness, and every plague, which is not written in the book of this law, them will the LORD bring upon thee, until thou be destroyed. And ye shall be left few in number, whereas ye were as the stars of heaven for multitude; because thou wouldest not obey the voice of the LORD thy God. And it shall come to pass, that as the LORD rejoiced over you to do you good, and to multiply you; so the LORD will rejoice over you to destroy you, and to bring you to nought; and ye shall be plucked from off the land whither thou goest to possess it.

[Rejoice! Rejoice! Rejoice!]

And the LORD shall scatter thee among all people, from the one end of the earth even unto the other; and there thou shalt serve other gods, which neither thou nor thy fathers have known, even wood and stone. And among these nations shalt thou find no ease, neither shall the sole of thy foot have rest: but the LORD shall give thee there a trembling heart, and failing of eyes, and sorrow of mind: And thy life shall hang in doubt before thee; and thou shalt fear day and night, and shalt have none assurance of thy life: In the morning thou shalt say, Would God it were even! and at even thou shalt say, Would God it were morning! for the fear of thine heart wherewith thou shalt fear, and for the sight of thine eyes which thou shalt see. And the LORD shall bring thee into Egypt again with ships, by the way whereof I spake unto thee, Thou shalt see it no more again: and there ye shall be sold unto your enemies for bondmen and bondwomen, and no man shall buy you.

Rejoice! Rejoice! Rejoice! Rejoice! Rejoice!
Why? Because God cared so much for us that He not only told us the blessings that He prepared for His children, He also told us what to do to keep them. Halleluiah!!

Because Bishop and Mother Hash taught God's Word line upon line and precept upon precept, the image of a poverty-stricken people changed to a progressive, successful people who could show the world the good, acceptable, and perfect will of God. The community and city leaders began to notice the success. You see, every person in the pews of your church is a voter and a taxpayer; thus the mayor's vision for the city becomes parallel with the vision of your church.

Repeat the growth cycle.
Bring them in…Teach them practical application of the Word…
Send them out
to tell others
Signs and wonders follow them that believe.

Close the back door
Sheep stay where they are fed and they'll go and tell others about the green pasture.

This is true evangelism and discipleship.

- Your church has the responsibility to help people keep balance in their lives.
- Develop methods to accomplish the same goal with fewer meetings and events.
- Empower families to give their talents back to God as well as serve their families and employers or run their own businesses.
- Be conscious of the community calendar as you set the church annual calendar.
- Collaborate with local colleges, schools, community organizations, and other churches.

If you own a business, you should ask yourself these questions:

1. What will make a person pass by ten other restaurants to get to mine?
2. What will make a person pass by ten other dry cleaners to get to mine, or a day care center, or any other business?"
3. How do people feel when they enter my parking lot or the foyer of my business?
4. What do they smell? What do they hear? What do they see?

So what makes a person pass by all the other churches that are on every block in the city to get to yours? People go and return to places where they have good experiences.

Evangelism and Discipleship Classes

Add an evangelism class to the Sunday Morning School of Ministry hour. The momentum of coming to Sunday morning classes will take root throughout the membership and will become a way of life. It will evolve to the point that sharing their testimony at their jobs, in the grocery store, on the tennis court, or wherever will become the norm. Growth will result and continue, because people want to be at a place where there is joy for their entire family. Your greatest advertisement is through word of mouth of happy, satisfied, changed people.

Accommodating Growth: Building a Bigger Sanctuary

> Enlarge the place of thy tent, and let them stretch forth the curtains of thine habitations: spare not, lengthen thy cords, and strengthen thy stakes...
> Isaiah 54:2

In the nineties, Bishop Hash formed the Research and Referral Committee to begin the search for land to build a church. The committee consisted of Herbert Allen, Cecilia Jones, Kay Slade, Gordon Slade, Delilah Miller, Elder J. C. Hash, and myself. After looking at many locations, the committee finally found a site that has a wonderful story behind it.

Mother Hash, the Dreamer

The Bible tells many stories of how God, through dreams, showed his servants what He had in store for them. Sometimes, He would warn them of trouble or to watch out for those who might spitefully use them, or to give instructions. Here is an example from God's Word.

> For God speaketh once, yea twice, yet man perceiveth it not. In a dream, in a vision of the night, when deep sleep falleth upon men, in slumberings upon the bed; Then he openeth the ears of men, and sealeth their instruction.
>
> Job 33:14-16

Mother Hash told of a dream she had in which she saw a great big open place that had a lot of red dirt. In her dream, she and a group of people were walking through this place and stumbled upon a glass case in which a beautiful woman was sleeping. When they opened the glass case, the woman opened her eyes and said, "Where have you been? I have been waiting for you for so long." When the committee took Mother Hash to see the land on Old Lexington Road, she instantly knew this was the place she saw in her dream.

The total vision was divided into three phases:

- Phase One - the multipurpose building that consisted of a 900-seat auditorium, offices, and classrooms for total family ministry.
- Phase Two - a building to house a 3,200-seat auditorium, media studio, bookstore, school, offices, and classrooms.
- Phase Three - a building for a Family Enrichment Center with two gymnasiums, a cafeteria, Bible College, classrooms, arcade, fitness center and more.

The committee did the research to find the owners of the land. We developed a professional presentation and traveled with Bishop Hash to California to request the land to be donated to St. Peter's to construct our building. While we were waiting for all of the legal transactions to be finalized for the contribution of the 55-acre land site, my brother, Elder J.C., conducted many prayer and communion services on the land. For more than a year, we waited for a response, but had not heard anything. One day, after he had finished praying, Elder J.C. called Gordon Slade, our accountant, and told him to call the office in California. Gordon was hesitant because the contact that he had been talking to did not seem to want to give him any attention. When Gordon called, it turned out that the man that was so hesitant was no longer in that position and the account had been turned over to someone else. God reached down all the way in California, moved someone out of the way, and miraculously the land was donated to us. Halleluiah!!!! We immediately began to put things in place to acquire the funds, contractors, and all the processes to begin our building. The entire congregation rejoiced and praised God for His mighty works.

The same thing that caused the explosive membership growth was used to finance the building: The Word of God and prayer manifested.

- The Word of God and prayer manifested in the daily lives of the people.
- The Word of God and prayer manifested in the finances of the people.
- The Word of God and prayer manifested in the businesses of the people.
- The Word of God and prayer manifested in the gifts and talents of the people.
  The entire congregation rejoiced and praised God for His mighty works.

This is the true picture of God's Church that we must show the world! No gimmicks or tricks, just teach people to live the God-kind of life, which is love, happiness, peace, and joy in the Holy Ghost. When their neighbor, co-worker, or sons and daughters see the God-kind of life demonstrated, they too will want to partake of God's goodness and then go and tell others.

CHAPTER SIX

Strategy Six

Look Beyond Your Congregation

"The Universal Church and the Local Body of Believers"

No Local Church Stands Alone.

Knowing that he could not carry God's vision alone, and that God has blessed the body of Christ with gifts in the form of men with specialized ministries, Bishop Hash made efforts to go beyond his congregation in providing ministry for his church and other churches around. This is a biblical principle that is demonstrated throughout the scriptures:

On the day of Pentecost, they were all with one accord!

And when the day of Pentecost was fully come, they were all with one accord in one place. And suddenly there came a sound from heaven as of a rushing mighty wind, and it filled all the house where they were sitting. And there appeared unto them cloven tongues like as of fire, and it sat upon each of them. And they were all filled with the Holy Ghost, and began to speak with other tongues, as the Spirit gave them utterance. *And there were dwelling at Jerusalem Jews, devout men, out of every nation under heaven.*

Now when this was noised abroad, the multitude came together, and were confounded, because that every man heard them speak in his own language. And they were all amazed and marvelled, saying one to another, Behold, are not all these which speak Galilaeans? And how hear we every man in our own tongue, wherein we were born? Parthians, and Medes, and Elamites, and the dwellers in Mesopotamia, and in Judaea, and Cappadocia, in Pontus, and Asia, Phrygia, and Pamphylia, in Egypt, and in the parts of Libya about Cyrene, and strangers of Rome, Jews and proselytes, Cretes and Arabians, we do hear them speak in our tongues the wonderful works of God.

And they were all amazed, and were in doubt, saying one to another, What meaneth this? Others mocking said, These men are full of new wine. But Peter, standing up with the eleven, lifted up his voice, and said unto them, Ye men of Judaea, and all ye that dwell at Jerusalem, be this known unto you, and hearken to my words: For these are not drunken, as ye suppose, seeing it is but the third hour of the day. But this is that which was spoken by the prophet Joel;

And it shall come to pass in the last days, saith God, I will pour out of my Spirit upon all flesh: and your sons and your daughters shall prophesy, and your young men shall see visions, and your old men shall dream dreams: And on my servants and on my handmaidens I will pour out in those days of my Spirit; and they shall prophesy: And I will shew wonders in heaven above, and signs in the earth beneath; blood, and fire, and vapour of smoke: The sun shall be turned into darkness, and the moon into blood, before the great and notable day of the Lord come: And it shall come to pass, that whosoever shall call on the name of the Lord shall be saved.

Acts 2:1-22

There are many ministerial organizations around, but if there is not one in your community, then start a covenant non-denominational ministerial organization by developing a relationship with the community pastors. Your organization's mission for the community is the same, which is to build the lives of God's people, not compare membership numbers. Iron sharpens iron, so learn from each other. As my granddaughter, Jade, says to her brother, Garic, "Don't hate, congratulate! Don't be jealous."

Jealousy and competition should never be among pastors; however, unfortunately it is. Like a revolving door, for years we have seen a trend of church hopping people.

Although there are thousands of people who have not received Jesus as their Lord and Savior, the devil has kept pastors fighting over members. The harvest is truly plentiful, but the laborers are few.

II Corinthians 2:11 instructs us not to be ignorant of the devil's devices and trickery lest Satan should get an advantage of us.

Lock in to what God has told you to do at your church. Do not compete with other ministries, just stick with what you should be doing. In the old days, people had to bring a letter from their former church before they could join a new church. With so many churches starting in American cities today, I think this might be a good strategy for us to use.

Collaboration and Affiliations

A buzzword that can be heard in the grant world is "collaboration." Get out of your four walls and share your vision with your local city mayor and other city officials. Collaborate with other community or national agencies and organizations to help build the lives of the people in your city. Charity begins at home and then spreads abroad. Before you put so much energy into becoming a world-renowned figure, concentrate on the humanitarian issues that are right in your own community.

The senior pastor and other leaders of the church should take advantage of the opportunity to serve on local and national boards that share your visions. Your women's, men's, youth's, and children's leaders should definitely represent your church and collaborate with other agencies and service organizations. After all, we are all in the same business, to win the lost at any cost. There is strength in unity!

The mission of any church is to develop God's people. There are enough people in *every* city for *every* pastor to fill *every* church!

Bishop Hash's Strategy: The Church of God Apostolic Conference

Bishop Hash sought to bring churches and ministries together through The Church of God Apostolic (COGA) National Conference. For nearly one hundred years, the Apostolic churches from all over the country met in Winston Salem for their annual General Assembly for their regional church reports.

Bishop Hash wanted to reflect his vision of the church beyond his congregation. He made a remarkable process at the conference by changing the existing format for ministry. Normally, the speakers for the conference were the Church of God Apostolic Board of Bishops, but one year, he decided to change the platform and invited Dr. Frederick K. C. Price of Crenshaw Christian Center in Inglewood, California to be the keynote speaker. Bishop Hash's wisdom told him that it had to be a Black man who was living the Word for his success in order for the COGA leaders to accept the change. It was a miracle because Dr. Price at that time did not know the Hashes, but he heard the voice of God and came to the conference two years in a row. Since then, he and his wife, Betty, have become lifelong friends of our family.

Bishop Hash wanted the conference attendees to return to their churches with solid principles and concepts for practical biblical application towards church growth, regardless of denominational affiliations.

In the following years, the speakers included renowned prophets, teachers, apostles, evangelists, and psalmists of God such as Kenneth Copeland, Kenneth Hagin, Sr., Larry Lee, Myles Munroe, Benson Idahosa, Phil Driscoll, Bill and Renae Morris, T.D. Jakes, Charles Capps and many more. Kenneth Copeland claims Mother Hash as his mama and stays in touch with her on a consistent basis.

Secondly, Bishop Hash opened the sessions to the public by conducting conferences on neutral ground at the Benton Convention Center in Winston Salem, NC so that people from all races and all denominations would feel free to come. He also did not charge a registration fee. Instead, on the first day of the conference he would inform the audience of the conference budget and believed God that the people would appreciate the expense and sacrifice, and support the conference with their offerings. The conferences were packed with five to ten thousand attendees each year and filled all of the hotels and restaurants in the Triad area. God always met the budget.

In fact, the National Black Theater Festival held its annual festival the same week as we did. We collaborated with them for several of the events during the week; therefore, many of the movie stars also attended our conference. It became an event that churches in the entire region (regardless of denomination) looked forward to attending each year.

The steps to goal (vision) setting that I previously mentioned detail how the concepts are handled. Once the vision is solidified, you start developing your organizational structure by asking yourself, "What are the skills needed to fulfill the vision?" Jethro told Moses to go and choose *able* men. The word able means qualified to do the work.

Moreover thou shalt provide out of all the people able men, such as fear God, men of truth, hating covetousness; and place such over them, to be rulers of thousands, and rulers of hundreds, rulers of fifties, and rulers of tens: And let them judge the people at all seasons: and it shall be, that every great matter they shall bring unto thee, but every small matter they shall judge: so shall it be easier for thyself, and they shall bear the burden with thee. If thou shalt do this thing, and God command thee so, then thou shalt be able to endure, and all this people shall also go to their place in peace.

Exodus 18:21-23

To summarize the processes for organizational structure and to keep it a simple process, I have developed this simple module. Notice the word *simple*.

Twelve Steps in Goal Setting

Another word for vision is G-O-A-L. How can you get others to connect with your vision to make it become a reality and their vision too? I have outlined simple graphs, modules, and other tools for successful business and ministry operations in my book entitled, *Building God's House – 200 Pages of Power to Succeed in Ministry*. God has given me a remarkable ability to hear a vision and then put a plan together from A-to-Z. I call it my "Z Factor". No matter how small or how large the project may be, these simple steps will work.

Don't be afraid to reach outside of your ministry to acquire the skilled staff you need. Once the vision for your ministry has been firmly established and presented to the people of the church, each department should work as a team to set short-, mid-, and long-term goals and strategies. The Administrator, Operations Director, or an outside consultant, usually facilitate these strategy sessions.

1. **Name your project or department**. Does the name reflect what you really do?
2. **Write your mission statement and vision**. This is extracted from the main vision of the church.

3. **Set goals.** Decide what needs to be done, develop a step-by-step plan, and set timelines for completing each. Take away excessive departments and programs that are not needed to fulfill the vision.
4. **Design your organizational flow chart** (leadership/staff structure). You must know what skills (the nuts and bolts) that are needed to complete the project. Avoid over staffing.
5. **Write one-page job descriptions** for each square on your organizational flow chart.
6. **Place loyal people with a passion** to be diligent in developing their square on the chart.
7. **Teach, train, and coach** each person on the chart. Review the mission frequently to keep everyone on one accord.
8. **Establish financial resources, avenues, and budgets** to support the project.
9. **Produce adequate facilities and technical equipment** to make the project functional.
10. **Establish an awards system** for immediate gratification. Pie in the sky in the sweet by and by is too far off for people to see. Give them their accolades while they can enjoy them.
11. **Establish an accountability system**, a reporting process. This allows for fixing roadblocks before they abort the project.
12. **Establish an evaluation module to obtain stats** (individually and corporately). This allows you to forecast processes for future growth.

I hope you notice that this plan involves many gifted, skilled people. The senior pastor cannot accomplish it alone. These steps create a spirit of ownership. People support a vision when they're aware of their place and know where they fit in. Like Aaron's robe, the plans must be precise and detailed.

Package the Vision and Stay Focused

Once these steps have been taken, package the plan, and then present your project to the leaders at a leadership meeting. Bathe your project in prayer and watch God do a miraculous work. Watch

Him bless the fruit of your labor. Have your marketing department create a professional presentation to present on a Sunday morning in the youth, children's, and adult services, so that your total congregation can buy into the plan. Stay focused and give quarterly reports to your congregation through a bulletin, newsletter, or PowerPoint presentation.

Build the *right team* and you will achieve *right results*.

CHAPTER SEVEN

Strategy Seven

Leave a Legacy

*"The vision of God is generational.
You must train a successor to carry
the vision on throughout the next generation?"*

Handover - The vision of God is generational. You must train a successor to carry the vision on throughout the next generation.

One day in 1989, Bishop Reuben K. Hash, Sr. stood in the pulpit at the church on Highland Avenue and began to summarize his sermon, when all of a sudden he turned to the congregation and began to prophesy instead. He told them how God was confirming that he was entering into a new season of his ministry and announced that he was retiring. Bishop Hash turned to his son, Elder J. C. Hash, Sr., and announced that he was turning the pastorship of the church over to him.

Yet now hear, O Jacob my servant; and Israel, whom I have chosen: Thus saith the LORD that made thee, and formed thee from the womb, which will help thee; Fear not, O Jacob, my servant; and thou, Jeshurun, whom I have chosen. For I will pour water upon him that is thirsty, and floods upon the dry ground: *I will pour my spirit upon thy seed, and my blessing upon thine offspring:* And they shall spring up as among the grass, as willows by the water courses.

Isaiah 44:1-4

Elder J.C. had worked diligently and faithfully with his father in implementing the changes at St. Peter's. Anything that anyone else would not do, he would do. He did not push to make a name for himself, and because of his faithfulness, God rewarded him. He often states today, that he is the least one that God could have chosen for this position. Elder J. C., who is now Dr., Bishop J.C. Hash, is a devout man of prayer and faith and strives wholeheartedly to live the Word of God to its fullest in order to be an example to his flock.

Bishop R. K. Hash, Sr. remained the General Overseer of the Church of God Apostolic. He continued to teach pastors the importance of knowing when to pass on the mantle wherever he went. He continued to teach and train pastors on solid church and business principles for church growth and traveled throughout the country. He also went to Nigeria, West Africa where he established fifteen churches and ordained pastors and an overseer for them. They were named the St. Reuben Church of God Apostolic.

Bishop Hash with the Board of Elders in Africa

Passing On

On June 17, 1993, five days before Mother Hash's birthday and exactly one month before their fifty-seventh wedding anniversary, Bishop Reuben K. Hash, Sr. expired this life on earth and is now enjoying eternal life with the Lord. He lived to be eighty-one years old and had the joy of seeing Phase One of the master plan completed.

At his home going celebration, resolutions and proclamations from mayors, governors, senators, and even the White House were received. Acknowledgements, cards, and telegrams were received from men of God like Kenneth Copeland, Kenneth Hagin, Sr., Fred Price, Oral Roberts, and several others. Many attended. There was not room enough to sit or to stand for all who desired to attend Bishop Hash's home going celebration.

Bishop Hash wrote his own eulogy throughout his life. His godly character, values and devout statue as a man of God radiated from everything that he touched. God's glory radiated from his life of helping people to become all that Jesus paid the price for them to become.

Every stone and every tree on the campus of St. Peter's World Outreach Center bares his spirit. One cannot help but remember him as they walk through the corridors and on the grounds. His life truly touched the lives of thousands.

Mother Hash is still preaching, praying, and praising God. She leads powerful noonday prayer services on Monday and Friday at St. Peter's. Many miraculous testimonies have come from those who attend the highly anointed prayer sessions. Often times, you will see her leading the prayer attendees across the campus to anoint every office and building as God leads her. We may never know how many spiritual attacks have been warded off from the church, the leaders, and families because of the prayers of Mother Hash and the noonday prayer warriors.

The Legacy Lives On

> One generation passeth away, and another generation cometh: but the earth abideth for ever.
>
> Ecclesiastes 1:4

Did the vision of the late Bishop R. K. Hash, Sr. cease when he expired this life on earth and made his passage to heaven? Absolutely not! His legacy lives on through his natural and spiritual sons and daughters who are pastoring growing churches and ministries throughout the nation. My brothers, Dr. Ronald Hash and Dr. Charles Hash, are pastoring flourishing churches in Roanoke, Virginia and East Spencer, NC. My brother, Bishop Leonard Hash, is serving the vision in Roanoke and Elder Reuben Hash is serving with my brother, Bishop J.C., at St. Peter's World Outreach Center along with my sister, Delilah. My oldest sister, Mamie, and her husband, Bishop Walter Anderson, pastor a church in Danville, Virginia.

All of my nieces and nephews are actively involved in ministry as well. They are highly gifted, talented singers, musicians, preachers, and most of, all they love the Lord. Although all of us have acquired several degrees and have been honored with great awards, the legacy of being servants in the kingdom of God defines who we really are.

I once read there are only two lasting bequests you can leave your children: roots, so they always know where they came from and wings, so they know how to fly.

Bishop Reuben K. and Mother Mildred Hash fulfilled both bequests. Through the foundation they built, St. Peter's church evolved from a small church in a basement to a three hundred-seat sanctuary to a 55-acre campus with a nine hundred-seat multipurpose gymnatorium, with classrooms and offices. Under their leadership, St. Peter's World Outreach Center became one of the most organized and tightly run ministries in the world. It is a model church that mentors, coaches, and trains pastors and leaders throughout the country.

My brother, Dr. J. C. Hash, Sr. and his wife, Joyce, are carrying the torch and have expanded St. Peter's World Outreach Center to become a world renowned ministry comprised of a 75-acre campus with over 150,000 square feet of buildings for total family and community outreach services and education. St. Peter's has the following amenities: a beautiful 3200 seat main auditorium, a family enrichment center with two Olympic-size gymnasiums with indoor walking tracks, a cafeteria, arcade, classrooms, a Bible college, daycare center, a 42-unit retirement home, a "We Care" community food and clothing center, and more. In his continual commitment to win souls and make disciples of men and women, Bishop J. C. Hash has transitioned St. Peter's World Outreach Center into a powerful and dynamic G-12 Network Cell Ministry.

When I took an early leave from full time daily work as Church Administrator on March 14, 2003, St. Peter's was run by twenty-two full and part time employees and over 800 volunteers who love the Lord with all their hearts and serve him diligently with their gifts, talents, and resources. Wherever I go to conduct seminars and workshops, I brag that I could put my neck on the chopping block knowing that come rain, snow, sleet, or shine, our volunteers were always in place every Sunday and any other day of the week, because they served God diligently for His diligence towards them.

The spirit and vision of Bishop R. K. and Mother Mildred Hash lives strong from generation to generation.

Forasmuch then as we are the offspring of God, we ought not to think that the Godhead is like unto gold, or silver, or stone, graven by art and man's device. And the times of this ignorance God winked at; but now commandeth all men every where to repent: Because he hath appointed a day, in the which he will judge the world in righteousness by that man whom he hath ordained; whereof he hath given assurance unto all men, in that he hath raised him from the dead.
Acts 17:29-31

Therefore, my brethren dearly beloved and longed for, my joy and crown, so stand fast in the Lord, my dearly beloved. I beseech Euodias, and beseech Syntyche, that they be of the same mind in the Lord. And I intreat thee also, true yokefellow, help those women which laboured with me in the gospel, with Clement also, and with other my fellow-labourers, whose names are in the book of life.

Rejoice in the Lord alway: and again I say, Rejoice. Let your moderation be known unto all men. The Lord is at hand.

Be careful for nothing; but in every thing by prayer and supplication with thanksgiving let your requests be made known unto God. And the peace of God, which passeth all understanding, shall keep your hearts and minds through Christ Jesus.

Finally, brethren, whatsoever things are true, whatsoever things are honest, whatsoever things are just, whatsoever things are pure, whatsoever things are lovely, whatsoever things are of good report; if there be any virtue, and if there be any praise, think on these things.
Philippians 4:1-8

In summary, it is very clear that God has given us specific strategies, a *master plan*, with every process and every nut and bolt, as to how to build His corporation, His Church. We must:

1. Understand God's vision for His Church.
2. Build people (spirit, soul, and body) because people are God's heartbeat.
3. Organize for the vision. Help people find where their gifts fit in the body of Christ.
4. Mobilize your church to pray because prayer is the power you need to put on the supernatural strength to accomplish the vision.
5. Evangelize for church growth because people must feel the reality of God in their daily lives.
6. Look beyond your congregation, because the whole earth belongs to God.
7. Leave a legacy, because God's vision is generational.

Building God's House – Seven Strategies for Raising a Healthy Church - The Reuben K. and Mildred T. Hash Story has touched on many principles and concepts for successful ministry operations. As Dr. Copland mentioned in the foreword, it would take volumes of books to tell the whole story of each strategy; however, each of them must be properly carried out if you desire to see your vision manifested in the natural during your life span on earth.

Do not leave for the next generation to do what God intended for you to do now. Leave the next generation with a legacy to build upon. Using these principles should provoke each generation to go higher and higher in the promises of God.

> And they shall be upon Aaron, and upon his sons, when they come in unto the tabernacle of the congregation, or when they come near unto the altar to minister in the holy place; that they bear not iniquity, and die: *it shall be a statute for ever unto him and his seed after him.*
> Exodus 28:43

Soar like an eagle. Surpass all of the secular corporations and show the world God's corporation as He truly has left us the master plan to follow.

The late Bishop Reuben K. Hash, Sr.
Mother Mildred Hash
Dr. Francene Hash

Appendix

Quotes of Wisdom by Mom and Dad Hash:

Boy!!! Let patience possess your soul! (Dad Hash)

Get in the Word and stay there, stay 'til Jesus comes. (Mother Hash)

The Holy Ghost is just like fire shut up in my bones! (Mother Hash)

Look a here. Do it right the first time. Then you won't waste your time, God's time, and everybody else's time having to do it over. (Dad Hash)

Smile Baby, Jesus loves you. (Mother Hash)

That's the God's honest truth. (Mother Hash)

Dad Hash's Favorite Hymnal Verses:

"When we've been there ten thousand years, bright shining as the sun. We've no less days to sing God's praise, then when we first begun."

"I shall not, I shall not be moved. Just like a tree planted by the water. I shall not be moved."

Mother Hash's Favorite Praise Songs:

"I'm a soldier in the army of the Lord. I'm a soldier in the army. Got my war clothes on. I'm on the battlefield. Got my sword in my hand in the army."

"He's a well of water in my soul. He's a well of water in my soul."

"God is a good God, yes He is."

"Real, real, Jesus is real to me. Oh yes, He gives me victory. So many people doubt Him, but I can't live without Him. That is why I love Him so; He's so real to me."

Bible References

All scripture is given by inspiration of God, and is profitable for doctrine, for reproof, for correction, for instruction in righteousness. That the man (woman) of God may be perfect, thoroughly furnished unto all good works.
II Timothy 3:16

Building God's House – Seven Strategies for Raising a Healthy Church was written to demonstrate that each step to run the Church of the Lord was given to us by our Father, God. To assist you in your study after you have read this book, listed below are the biblical Scripture references within each chapter:

Strategy One – Understand God's Vision for the Church
Exodus 3:16-17
Exodus 28:1-5
Exodus 28:6-43
Ephesians 4:10-16
Ephesians 5:25-27
Revelations 7:9-17
Ephesians 4:13
Habakkuk 2:14
Revelations 7:14
Acts 20:28
I Peter 5:1-4

John 21:15-17
Habakkuk 2:1-3

***God's Vision in a Man's Heart -
"The R.K. and Mildred T. Hash Story"***
I Corinthians 11:15
Exodus 3:7-10
Nehemiah 1:1-3
Nehemiah 2:1-4
Mark 10:45
II Timothy 3:16-17
Psalms 37:1-8
Genesis 1:1-5

Strategy Two – Build People: The Heartbeat of God's Vision
Hosea 4:6
Ezekiel 34:1-6
Matthew 18:10-14
Matthew 23:15
Matthew 18:6
Matthew 4:4
Luke 4:4
Hebrew 11:1-25
Hosea 4:6
Malachi 3:10
Mark 12:17
Luke 20:25
I Corinthians 12:22-23
III John 3
Deuteronomy 28
Hebrews 6:1-20
I Kings 17:2-16
Exodus 18:19-22
Exodus 18:14
I Corinthians 12:4-26
Ecclesiastes 3:1-22

Strategy Three – Organize for the Vision
Psalms 68:11
Ephesians 4:11-12
Exodus 18:13-22
Acts 6:1-7
Ephesians 4:10-13
I Corinthians 12:27-31
I Corinthians 13
Luke 6:38
I Corinthians 12
Romans 12
Ephesians 4
I Corinthians 12:1-27
I Corinthians 12:28
Ephesians 4:11-16
Luke 6:46-49
Matthew 16:13-19
Luke 15:1-6
Romans 12:11
Proverbs 22:29
Acts 6:3
Isaiah 6:3
Psalms 24:1-2
Psalms 126:2-3
Isaiah 12:3-6

Strategy Four – Mobilize Your Church to Pray –
"Power for the Vision"
I Thessalonians 5:14-18
Matthew 6:1-13
Genesis 1:1-31
Genesis 2:1-25
Psalms 122:6
Matthew 5:44
James 5:13-15
James 5:16
Ephesians 6:18

I Timothy 2:1-2
Philippians 4:6
I John 5:14-15
I Peter 5:1-6
Titus 2:2-8
I Timothy 5:1-2

Strategy Five – Evangelize for Church Growth
Proverbs 11:30
Matthew 9:35-38
Matthew 10:6-7
Matthew 4:18-22
Mark 1:17
Luke 5:31-32
Matthew 8:17-19
Luke 9:56-57
Matthew 28:18-20
I Timothy 2:4-6
Matthew 18:10-14
Luke 15:1-7
Galatians 5:16-26
Deuteronomy 28:1-13
Deuteronomy 28:14-65
Isaiah 54:2
Job 33:14-16

Strategy Six – Look Beyond Your Congregation
Acts 2:1-22
II Corinthians 2:11
Exodus 18:21-23

Strategy Seven – Leave a Legacy
Isaiah 44:1-4
Ecclesiastes 1:4
Acts 17:29-31
Philippians 4:1-8
Exodus 28:43

Footnote: "The Vision Thing" by Chris Lee, Training the Human Side of Business, Volume 30, Number 2, February, 1993. The Henry Ford Vision

Footnote: Operations Manual, St. Peter's World Outreach Center

Epilogue

Dr. Francene Hash is tops in her field. Coming from four generations of preachers, she has been active in church administration and management most of her adult life. She is one of twelve children of the world-renowned preachers and teachers, the late Bishop Reuben K. Hash, Sr. and Mother Mildred T. Hash, who nurtured, molded, and developed all of their children to be steadfast and grounded in the work of the Lord.

All of her life, Dr. Hash traveled with her parents to church conferences, sang at revivals, and learned how to do mostly anything that needed to be done in the church. During a period of fourteen months, her mother was recovering from a severe illness in a hospital that was over three hundred miles from the small town where they lived. Bishop Hash took Francene to every local ministerial meeting and to other social functions with him. Most of the time, she was the only child present, but she didn't mind because with her mom being so far away, her daddy was her security. Thus, all of these experiences prepared her for the work in church administration that later came in her life.

In 1977, Dr. Hash moved to Winston Salem, North Carolina to teach school and to pursue a career in education. She also assisted her father in his church and in 1989; she became the first full time Church Administrator of St. Peter's World Outreach Center that has grown to be a large membership of over three thousand five hundred people. It is a multifaceted, multiethnic ministry established with a sound operational structure. Dr. Hash had the responsibility of overseeing through a delegatory structure, all ministries and departments of the church. Because of the tremendous surge of growth and the order and structure of how the ministry operates at St. Peter's World Outreach Center, the demand for Dr. Hash to conduct workshops and to speak all over the country increased to the degree that it demanded her to put her life's experience in church administration into two outstanding books, *Building God's House- Seven Strategies for Raising a Healthy Church. The Reuben K. and Mildred T. Hash Story* and *Building God's House Resource Book – 200 Pages of Power to Succeed in Ministry*. These books have inspired other books that are in the process of being written about successful church ministry operations. Watch for them in your local bookstores.

Dr. Hash is a graduate of Radford University in Radford, Virginia with a Bachelor of Science degree in Early Childhood Education and Education for the Mentally Handicapped. She attended business administration classes at Forsyth Technical Institute in Winston Salem, NC and graduate school at Gardner Webb University in Boone, North Carolina. In 2004, she received an honorary doctorate degree from New Life Theological Seminary of Orangeburg, SC.

Her collections of writings have grown from poems to short stories to novels and she comes to the world as an author, teacher, lecturer, motivational speaker, trainer, executive facilitator, and consultant.

Additional Information About Dr. Hash
- Founder and CEO of The Church Growth Coalition Training Institute, Inc. and Executive Management, Inc.
- National Conference Speaker
- An ordained teacher of the gospel
- Member of the National Association of Fund Raisers
- Member of the National Religious Conference Management Association
- Alumni member of Leadership Winston-Salem and Leadership Connections
- Actively involved in numerous community organizations

- Former elementary school teacher for eleven years
- Proud mother of two wonderful children and two outstanding grandchildren

Acknowledgments

Two of the greatest gifts God has ever given to mankind are family and friends. This book was made possible because God put so many wonderful, true family members, and friends in my life.

Thanks to my children, Sean and Tameeka, who have allowed their mom to divide their time to serve so many others and yet they still grew up to be such a fine young man and woman. I am so proud of what God has made out of you. Tameeka, thanks for my two beautiful grandchildren, Jade Renae' and Garic JaVon. Sean, your demonstration of honesty and integrity makes me proud that you're my son.

Honor to my dad, the late Bishop Reuben K. Hash, Sr. who made me know that I was his princess and filled me with values and strength that have carried me throughout my life.

Love to my two moms, my big sister Delilah Miller, and my mama, Mother Mildred T. Hash. Through thick and thin you both have always been there for me, praying for me, and encouraging me to be strong.

To Alexandria Smith, Linda Whelan, Pat Stepney, Nancy Hash, Mother Abbott, and Chandra Stewart – you *never* stop supporting me!!! Repeatedly you unselfishly give me your expertise and skills to make me look good. The words "Thank you" could never begin to express how deeply appreciative I am to you for your love.

And thanks to all the other angels that God placed in my path, too many to name, who have been Aarons and Hurs to hold up my arms to complete this project. To Dr. Cephas Narh, thank you for your recommendations that helped me take the words from my heart and project my message to the world. Your skills are such a blessing to the body of Christ.

To my brothers and sisters, Dr. J. C. Hash, Dr. Charles Hash, Dr. Ronald Hash, Bishop Leonard Hash, Elder Reuben Hash, and Pastor Mamie Anderson, Eugene, Chris, and Swanson, thank you for praying for me and encouraging me to develop the work that God created on the inside of me for the entire body of Christ.

To all of my beautiful cousins, nieces, nephews, aunts and uncles, I love you so much.

AND MOST OF ALL ...Thank you Heavenly Father for your goodness and mercy to me. I will always lift my voice to Thee and magnify your Holy name.

About the Resource Book

ABOUT THE RESOURCE BOOK

Dr. Francene Hash has written a resource book on church management that explains step by step how to organize and structure a ministry vision for total success. *Building God's House Resource Book – 200 Pages of Power to Succeed in Ministry* comes in a power-packed simple format with reproducible templates, forms, and charts:

Section One......Visions from God
Section Two......The Gifts Are in the House
Section Three... Organization and Structure of the Gifts
Section Four......Training, Accountability, and Evaluation
Section Five.......Administration – Order, Policies & Procedures

A Brief Synopsis of Each Section

Section One - Visions from God

God gives leaders a vision, however, if a leader does not establish the vision using the tools and principles established in God's Word, the vision will tarry. This section shows how to write the vision and make it plain.

Section Two - The Gifts are in the House

When God gives a vision, He will equip you with the necessary people to accomplish the vision. This section shows how to stir up the gifts that are created on the inside of every believer for the work of the ministry. There's power in the pews.

Section Three - Organization and Structure of the Gifts

In Exodus 18, Jethro instructed Moses to choose some *able* men to help him oversee the children of Israel. Likewise, pastors must select able leaders and place them over the various departments to train and develop the gifts in the people under them. This section shows how to organize the volunteer and paid staff for maximum success.

Section Four - Training, Accountability, and Evaluation

Invest in your people and your people will invest in your ministry. This section demonstrates the process of reproduction of the gifts to keep up with the growth of the church in serving the needs of the congregation.

Section Five – Administration – Order, Policies & Procedures

So that everyone in the church may speak the same thing, establish written policies and procedures to govern the entire operation of the ministry. This section shows how to write operations manuals, policies and procedures, and how to measure the growth to forecast future long-term planning.

Dr. Francene Hash,
Founder/CEO/President

Through the Church Growth Coalition Training Institute, Inc., Dr. Hash is available to speak at conferences and to conduct leadership seminars and workshops. The Church Growth Coalition also offers consultation to visionaries in designing their master plan and all aspects of ministry operations.

Contact Information:
www.fhtmus.com/francene

Imagine a place where people diligently run to give their talents and services to the Lord.
Imagine a place where people gladly come early and stay late to help others.
Imagine a place where people freely give above and beyond their tithes and offerings.

This place must be your church!
Think on these things!

Dr. Francene Hash is tops in her field. Coming from four generations of preachers, she has been active in church administration and management most of her adult life. For more than twenty-six years, she has written operations manuals for practically everything there could possibly be about church ministry and business operations. Her success in administration and leadership has developed a reputation whereby she is known throughout the country to be an expert in her field. She comes to the world as an author, teacher, lecturer, motivational speaker, leadership trainer, executive facilitator, and consultant.

When the late Bishop R. K. Hash hired me as his accountant, I can't describe the honor that I felt to be chosen by such a devout man of integrity to perform such a vital function for the Lord. This appointment gave me the pleasure to work with Dr. Francene who has a profound leadership style and a keen skill as a team developer. It is a joy to watch her administrative skills in action and to see her passion to hear a vision, and then to chart out every detail step by step. Dr. Francene is truly a gift to the body of Christ! *She is the epitome of ministry in excellence!*

Gordon Slade, CPA

As a financial professional, I am continually looking for information to help me help others. After having read *Building God's House* by Dr. Francene Hash, I have found a resource that is invaluable to gain the knowledge that will make a difference when working with others to achieve their goals. Through God and His Word, with the help of Dr. Francene's book, it is now possible to make the changes to make growth possible.

Lindsay S. Loflin, Sr., RHU, LUTC
Financial Professional

CPSIA information can be obtained at www.ICGtesting.com
Printed in the USA
BVOW032357040712

294311BV00001B/5/A